CAREER EXAMINATION SERIES

THIS IS YOUR **PASSBOOK**® FOR ...

MATERIEL CONTROL CLERK III

NLC®

NATIONAL LEARNING CORPORATION®
passbooks.com

COPYRIGHT NOTICE

This book is SOLELY intended for, is sold ONLY to, and its use is RESTRICTED to individual, bona fide applicants or candidates who qualify by virtue of having seriously filed applications for appropriate license, certificate, professional and/or promotional advancement, higher school matriculation, scholarship, or other legitimate requirements of educational and/or governmental authorities.

This book is NOT intended for use, class instruction, tutoring, training, duplication, copying, reprinting, excerption, or adaptation, etc., by:

1) Other publishers
2) Proprietors and/or Instructors of «Coaching» and/or Preparatory Courses
3) Personnel and/or Training Divisions of commercial, industrial, and governmental organizations
4) Schools, colleges, or universities and/or their departments and staffs, including teachers and other personnel
5) Testing Agencies or Bureaus
6) Study groups which seek by the purchase of a single volume to copy and/or duplicate and/or adapt this material for use by the group as a whole without having purchased individual volumes for each of the members of the group
7) Et al.

Such persons would be in violation of appropriate Federal and State statutes.

PROVISION OF LICENSING AGREEMENTS. — Recognized educational, commercial, industrial, and governmental institutions and organizations, and others legitimately engaged in educational pursuits, including training, testing, and measurement activities, may address request for a licensing agreement to the copyright owners, who will determine whether, and under what conditions, including fees and charges, the materials in this book may be used them. In other words, a licensing facility exists for the legitimate use of the material in this book on other than an individual basis. However, it is asseverated and affirmed here that the material in this book CANNOT be used without the receipt of the express permission of such a licensing agreement from the Publishers. Inquiries re licensing should be addressed to the company, attention rights and permissions department.

All rights reserved, including the right of reproduction in whole or in part, in any form or by any means, electronic or mechanical, including photocopying, recording, or by any information storage and retrieval system, without permission in writing from the Publisher.

Copyright © 2018 by

NLC®

National Learning Corporation

212 Michael Drive, Syosset, NY 11791
(516) 921-8888 • www.passbooks.com
E-mail: info@passbooks.com

PUBLISHED IN THE UNITED STATES OF AMERICA

PASSBOOK® SERIES

THE *PASSBOOK® SERIES* has been created to prepare applicants and candidates for the ultimate academic battlefield – the examination room.

At some time in our lives, each and every one of us may be required to take an examination – for validation, matriculation, admission, qualification, registration, certification, or licensure.

Based on the assumption that every applicant or candidate has met the basic formal educational standards, has taken the required number of courses, and read the necessary texts, the *PASSBOOK® SERIES* furnishes the one special preparation which may assure passing with confidence, instead of failing with insecurity. Examination questions – together with answers – are furnished as the basic vehicle for study so that the mysteries of the examination and its compounding difficulties may be eliminated or diminished by a sure method.

This book is meant to help you pass your examination provided that you qualify and are serious in your objective.

The entire field is reviewed through the huge store of content information which is succinctly presented through a provocative and challenging approach – the question-and-answer method.

A climate of success is established by furnishing the correct answers at the end of each test.

You soon learn to recognize types of questions, forms of questions, and patterns of questioning. You may even begin to anticipate expected outcomes.

You perceive that many questions are repeated or adapted so that you can gain acute insights, which may enable you to score many sure points.

You learn how to confront new questions, or types of questions, and to attack them confidently and work out the correct answers.

You note objectives and emphases, and recognize pitfalls and dangers, so that you may make positive educational adjustments.

Moreover, you are kept fully informed in relation to new concepts, methods, practices, and directions in the field.

You discover that you arre actually taking the examination all the time: you are preparing for the examination by "taking" an examination, not by reading extraneous and/or supererogatory textbooks.

In short, this PASSBOOK®, used directedly, should be an important factor in helping you to pass your test.

MATERIEL CONTROL CLERK III

DUTIES
Performs complex record keeping and routine manual tasks in receiving, labeling, counting, sorting, storing, and transporting a variety of supplies, equipment, furnishings, and mail. Maintains perpetual inventory of warehoused material; keeps cumulative totals by several variables. Keeps accounts of charges against budget code of consumer; may use adding machine or typewriter to verify calculations or post headings on accounts and logs. May supervise subordinate level Materiel Control Clerks, Warehouse Workers, Laborers, and other personnel performing manual or clerical duties in the facility. Performs related work as required.

SUBJECT OF EXAMINATION
The written test will be designed to cover knowledge, skills, and/or abilities in such areas as:
1. Storeskeeping and inventory control;
2. Keeping simple inventory records;
3. Name and number checking;
4. Interpreting written directions;
5. Organizing data into tables and records; and
6. Supervision.

HOW TO TAKE A TEST

I. YOU MUST PASS AN EXAMINATION

A. WHAT EVERY CANDIDATE SHOULD KNOW

Examination applicants often ask us for help in preparing for the written test. What can I study in advance? What kinds of questions will be asked? How will the test be given? How will the papers be graded?

As an applicant for a civil service examination, you may be wondering about some of these things. Our purpose here is to suggest effective methods of advance study and to describe civil service examinations.

Your chances for success on this examination can be increased if you know how to prepare. Those "pre-examination jitters" can be reduced if you know what to expect. You can even experience an adventure in good citizenship if you know why civil service exams are given.

B. WHY ARE CIVIL SERVICE EXAMINATIONS GIVEN?

Civil service examinations are important to you in two ways. As a citizen, you want public jobs filled by employees who know how to do their work. As a job seeker, you want a fair chance to compete for that job on an equal footing with other candidates. The best-known means of accomplishing this two-fold goal is the competitive examination.

Exams are widely publicized throughout the nation. They may be administered for jobs in federal, state, city, municipal, town or village governments or agencies.

Any citizen may apply, with some limitations, such as the age or residence of applicants. Your experience and education may be reviewed to see whether you meet the requirements for the particular examination. When these requirements exist, they are reasonable and applied consistently to all applicants. Thus, a competitive examination may cause you some uneasiness now, but it is your privilege and safeguard.

C. HOW ARE CIVIL SERVICE EXAMS DEVELOPED?

Examinations are carefully written by trained technicians who are specialists in the field known as "psychological measurement," in consultation with recognized authorities in the field of work that the test will cover. These experts recommend the subject matter areas or skills to be tested; only those knowledges or skills important to your success on the job are included. The most reliable books and source materials available are used as references. Together, the experts and technicians judge the difficulty level of the questions.

Test technicians know how to phrase questions so that the problem is clearly stated. Their ethics do not permit "trick" or "catch" questions. Questions may have been tried out on sample groups, or subjected to statistical analysis, to determine their usefulness.

Written tests are often used in combination with performance tests, ratings of training and experience, and oral interviews. All of these measures combine to form the best-known means of finding the right person for the right job.

II. HOW TO PASS THE WRITTEN TEST

A. NATURE OF THE EXAMINATION

To prepare intelligently for civil service examinations, you should know how they differ from school examinations you have taken. In school you were assigned certain definite pages to read or subjects to cover. The examination questions were quite detailed and usually emphasized memory. Civil service exams, on the other hand, try to discover your present ability to perform the duties of a position, plus your potentiality to learn these duties. In other words, a civil service exam attempts to predict how successful you will be. Questions cover such a broad area that they cannot be as minute and detailed as school exam questions.

In the public service similar kinds of work, or positions, are grouped together in one "class." This process is known as *position-classification*. All the positions in a class are paid according to the salary range for that class. One class title covers all of these positions, and they are all tested by the same examination.

B. FOUR BASIC STEPS

1) Study the announcement

How, then, can you know what subjects to study? Our best answer is: "Learn as much as possible about the class of positions for which you've applied." The exam will test the knowledge, skills and abilities needed to do the work.

Your most valuable source of information about the position you want is the official exam announcement. This announcement lists the training and experience qualifications. Check these standards and apply only if you come reasonably close to meeting them.

The brief description of the position in the examination announcement offers some clues to the subjects which will be tested. Think about the job itself. Review the duties in your mind. Can you perform them, or are there some in which you are rusty? Fill in the blank spots in your preparation.

Many jurisdictions preview the written test in the exam announcement by including a section called "Knowledge and Abilities Required," "Scope of the Examination," or some similar heading. Here you will find out specifically what fields will be tested.

2) Review your own background

Once you learn in general what the position is all about, and what you need to know to do the work, ask yourself which subjects you already know fairly well and which need improvement. You may wonder whether to concentrate on improving your strong areas or on building some background in your fields of weakness. When the announcement has specified "some knowledge" or "considerable knowledge," or has used adjectives like "beginning principles of..." or "advanced ... methods," you can get a clue as to the number and difficulty of questions to be asked in any given field. More questions, and hence broader coverage, would be included for those subjects which are more important in the work. Now weigh your strengths and weaknesses against the job requirements and prepare accordingly.

3) Determine the level of the position

Another way to tell how intensively you should prepare is to understand the level of the job for which you are applying. Is it the entering level? In other words, is this the position in which beginners in a field of work are hired? Or is it an intermediate or advanced level? Sometimes this is indicated by such words as "Junior" or "Senior" in the class title. Other jurisdictions use Roman numerals to designate the level – Clerk I, Clerk II, for example. The word "Supervisor" sometimes appears in the title. If the level is not indicated by the title, check the description of duties. Will you be working under very close supervision, or will you have responsibility for independent decisions in this work?

4) Choose appropriate study materials

Now that you know the subjects to be examined and the relative amount of each subject to be covered, you can choose suitable study materials. For beginning level jobs, or even advanced ones, if you have a pronounced weakness in some aspect of your training, read a modern, standard textbook in that field. Be sure it is up to date and has general coverage. Such books are normally available at your library, and the librarian will be glad to help you locate one. For entry-level positions, questions of appropriate difficulty are chosen – neither highly advanced questions, nor those too simple. Such questions require careful thought but not advanced training.

If the position for which you are applying is technical or advanced, you will read more advanced, specialized material. If you are already familiar with the basic principles of your field, elementary textbooks would waste your time. Concentrate on advanced textbooks and technical periodicals. Think through the concepts and review difficult problems in your field.

These are all general sources. You can get more ideas on your own initiative, following these leads. For example, training manuals and publications of the government agency which employs workers in your field can be useful, particularly for technical and professional positions. A letter or visit to the government department involved may result in more specific study suggestions, and certainly will provide you with a more definite idea of the exact nature of the position you are seeking.

III. KINDS OF TESTS

Tests are used for purposes other than measuring knowledge and ability to perform specified duties. For some positions, it is equally important to test ability to make adjustments to new situations or to profit from training. In others, basic mental abilities not dependent on information are essential. Questions which test these things may not appear as pertinent to the duties of the position as those which test for knowledge and information. Yet they are often highly important parts of a fair examination. For very general questions, it is almost impossible to help you direct your study efforts. What we can do is to point out some of the more common of these general abilities needed in public service positions and describe some typical questions.

1) General information

Broad, general information has been found useful for predicting job success in some kinds of work. This is tested in a variety of ways, from vocabulary lists to questions about current events. Basic background in some field of work, such as sociology or economics, may be sampled in a group of questions. Often these are principles which have become familiar to most persons through exposure rather than through formal training. It is difficult to advise you how to study for these questions; being alert to the world around you is our best suggestion.

2) Verbal ability

An example of an ability needed in many positions is verbal or language ability. Verbal ability is, in brief, the ability to use and understand words. Vocabulary and grammar tests are typical measures of this ability. Reading comprehension or paragraph interpretation questions are common in many kinds of civil service tests. You are given a paragraph of written material and asked to find its central meaning.

3) Numerical ability

Number skills can be tested by the familiar arithmetic problem, by checking paired lists of numbers to see which are alike and which are different, or by interpreting charts and graphs. In the latter test, a graph may be printed in the test booklet which you are asked to use as the basis for answering questions.

4) Observation

A popular test for law-enforcement positions is the observation test. A picture is shown to you for several minutes, then taken away. Questions about the picture test your ability to observe both details and larger elements.

5) Following directions

In many positions in the public service, the employee must be able to carry out written instructions dependably and accurately. You may be given a chart with several columns, each column listing a variety of information. The questions require you to carry out directions involving the information given in the chart.

6) Skills and aptitudes

Performance tests effectively measure some manual skills and aptitudes. When the skill is one in which you are trained, such as typing or shorthand, you can practice. These tests are often very much like those given in business school or high school courses. For many of the other skills and aptitudes, however, no short-time preparation can be made. Skills and abilities natural to you or that you have developed throughout your lifetime are being tested.

Many of the general questions just described provide all the data needed to answer the questions and ask you to use your reasoning ability to find the answers. Your best preparation for these tests, as well as for tests of facts and ideas, is to be at your physical and mental best. You, no doubt, have your own methods of getting into an exam-taking mood and keeping "in shape." The next section lists some ideas on this subject.

IV. KINDS OF QUESTIONS

Only rarely is the "essay" question, which you answer in narrative form, used in civil service tests. Civil service tests are usually of the short-answer type. Full instructions for answering these questions will be given to you at the examination. But in case this is your first experience with short-answer questions and separate answer sheets, here is what you need to know:

1) Multiple-choice Questions

Most popular of the short-answer questions is the "multiple choice" or "best answer" question. It can be used, for example, to test for factual knowledge, ability to solve problems or judgment in meeting situations found at work.

A multiple-choice question is normally one of three types—
- It can begin with an incomplete statement followed by several possible endings. You are to find the one ending which *best* completes the statement, although some of the others may not be entirely wrong.
- It can also be a complete statement in the form of a question which is answered by choosing one of the statements listed.
- It can be in the form of a problem – again you select the best answer.

Here is an example of a multiple-choice question with a discussion which should give you some clues as to the method for choosing the right answer:

When an employee has a complaint about his assignment, the action which will *best* help him overcome his difficulty is to
   A. discuss his difficulty with his coworkers
   B. take the problem to the head of the organization
   C. take the problem to the person who gave him the assignment
   D. say nothing to anyone about his complaint

In answering this question, you should study each of the choices to find which is best. Consider choice "A" – Certainly an employee may discuss his complaint with fellow employees, but no change or improvement can result, and the complaint remains unresolved. Choice "B" is a poor choice since the head of the organization probably does not know what assignment you have been given, and taking your problem to him is known as "going over the head" of the supervisor. The supervisor, or person who made the assignment, is the person who can clarify it or correct any injustice. Choice "C" is, therefore, correct. To say nothing, as in choice "D," is unwise. Supervisors have and interest in knowing the problems employees are facing, and the employee is seeking a solution to his problem.

2) True/False Questions

The "true/false" or "right/wrong" form of question is sometimes used. Here a complete statement is given. Your job is to decide whether the statement is right or wrong.

SAMPLE: A roaming cell-phone call to a nearby city costs less than a non-roaming call to a distant city.

This statement is wrong, or false, since roaming calls are more expensive.
This is not a complete list of all possible question forms, although most of the others are variations of these common types. You will always get complete directions for

answering questions. Be sure you understand *how* to mark your answers – ask questions until you do.

V. RECORDING YOUR ANSWERS

Computer terminals are used more and more today for many different kinds of exams.

For an examination with very few applicants, you may be told to record your answers in the test booklet itself. Separate answer sheets are much more common. If this separate answer sheet is to be scored by machine – and this is often the case – it is highly important that you mark your answers correctly in order to get credit.

An electronic scoring machine is often used in civil service offices because of the speed with which papers can be scored. Machine-scored answer sheets must be marked with a pencil, which will be given to you. This pencil has a high graphite content which responds to the electronic scoring machine. As a matter of fact, stray dots may register as answers, so do not let your pencil rest on the answer sheet while you are pondering the correct answer. Also, if your pencil lead breaks or is otherwise defective, ask for another.

Since the answer sheet will be dropped in a slot in the scoring machine, be careful not to bend the corners or get the paper crumpled.

The answer sheet normally has five vertical columns of numbers, with 30 numbers to a column. These numbers correspond to the question numbers in your test booklet. After each number, going across the page are four or five pairs of dotted lines. These short dotted lines have small letters or numbers above them. The first two pairs may also have a "T" or "F" above the letters. This indicates that the first two pairs only are to be used if the questions are of the true-false type. If the questions are multiple choice, disregard the "T" and "F" and pay attention only to the small letters or numbers.

Answer your questions in the manner of the sample that follows:

32. The largest city in the United States is
    A. Washington, D.C.
    B. New York City
    C. Chicago
    D. Detroit
    E. San Francisco

1) Choose the answer you think is best. (New York City is the largest, so "B" is correct.)
2) Find the row of dotted lines numbered the same as the question you are answering. (Find row number 32)
3) Find the pair of dotted lines corresponding to the answer. (Find the pair of lines under the mark "B.")
4) Make a solid black mark between the dotted lines.

VI. BEFORE THE TEST

Common sense will help you find procedures to follow to get ready for an examination. Too many of us, however, overlook these sensible measures. Indeed, nervousness and fatigue have been found to be the most serious reasons why applicants fail to do their best on civil service tests. Here is a list of reminders:

- Begin your preparation early – Don't wait until the last minute to go scurrying around for books and materials or to find out what the position is all about.
- Prepare continuously – An hour a night for a week is better than an all-night cram session. This has been definitely established. What is more, a night a week for a month will return better dividends than crowding your study into a shorter period of time.
- Locate the place of the exam – You have been sent a notice telling you when and where to report for the examination. If the location is in a different town or otherwise unfamiliar to you, it would be well to inquire the best route and learn something about the building.
- Relax the night before the test – Allow your mind to rest. Do not study at all that night. Plan some mild recreation or diversion; then go to bed early and get a good night's sleep.
- Get up early enough to make a leisurely trip to the place for the test – This way unforeseen events, traffic snarls, unfamiliar buildings, etc. will not upset you.
- Dress comfortably – A written test is not a fashion show. You will be known by number and not by name, so wear something comfortable.
- Leave excess paraphernalia at home – Shopping bags and odd bundles will get in your way. You need bring only the items mentioned in the official notice you received; usually everything you need is provided. Do not bring reference books to the exam. They will only confuse those last minutes and be taken away from you when in the test room.
- Arrive somewhat ahead of time – If because of transportation schedules you must get there very early, bring a newspaper or magazine to take your mind off yourself while waiting.
- Locate the examination room – When you have found the proper room, you will be directed to the seat or part of the room where you will sit. Sometimes you are given a sheet of instructions to read while you are waiting. Do not fill out any forms until you are told to do so; just read them and be prepared.
- Relax and prepare to listen to the instructions
- If you have any physical problem that may keep you from doing your best, be sure to tell the test administrator. If you are sick or in poor health, you really cannot do your best on the exam. You can come back and take the test some other time.

VII. AT THE TEST

The day of the test is here and you have the test booklet in your hand. The temptation to get going is very strong. Caution! There is more to success than knowing the right answers. You must know how to identify your papers and understand variations in the type of short-answer question used in this particular examination. Follow these suggestions for maximum results from your efforts:

1) Cooperate with the monitor

The test administrator has a duty to create a situation in which you can be as much at ease as possible. He will give instructions, tell you when to begin, check to see that you are marking your answer sheet correctly, and so on. He is not there to guard you, although he will see that your competitors do not take unfair advantage. He wants to help you do your best.

2) Listen to all instructions

Don't jump the gun! Wait until you understand all directions. In most civil service tests you get more time than you need to answer the questions. So don't be in a hurry. Read each word of instructions until you clearly understand the meaning. Study the examples, listen to all announcements and follow directions. Ask questions if you do not understand what to do.

3) Identify your papers

Civil service exams are usually identified by number only. You will be assigned a number; you must not put your name on your test papers. Be sure to copy your number correctly. Since more than one exam may be given, copy your exact examination title.

4) Plan your time

Unless you are told that a test is a "speed" or "rate of work" test, speed itself is usually not important. Time enough to answer all the questions will be provided, but this does not mean that you have all day. An overall time limit has been set. Divide the total time (in minutes) by the number of questions to determine the approximate time you have for each question.

5) Do not linger over difficult questions

If you come across a difficult question, mark it with a paper clip (useful to have along) and come back to it when you have been through the booklet. One caution if you do this – be sure to skip a number on your answer sheet as well. Check often to be sure that you have not lost your place and that you are marking in the row numbered the same as the question you are answering.

6) Read the questions

Be sure you know what the question asks! Many capable people are unsuccessful because they failed to *read* the questions correctly.

7) Answer all questions

Unless you have been instructed that a penalty will be deducted for incorrect answers, it is better to guess than to omit a question.

8) Speed tests

It is often better NOT to guess on speed tests. It has been found that on timed tests people are tempted to spend the last few seconds before time is called in marking answers at random – without even reading them – in the hope of picking up a few extra points. To discourage this practice, the instructions may warn you that your score will be "corrected" for guessing. That is, a penalty will be applied. The incorrect answers will be deducted from the correct ones, or some other penalty formula will be used.

9) Review your answers

If you finish before time is called, go back to the questions you guessed or omitted to give them further thought. Review other answers if you have time.

10) Return your test materials

If you are ready to leave before others have finished or time is called, take ALL your materials to the monitor and leave quietly. Never take any test material with you. The monitor can discover whose papers are not complete, and taking a test booklet may be grounds for disqualification.

VIII. EXAMINATION TECHNIQUES

1) Read the general instructions carefully. These are usually printed on the first page of the exam booklet. As a rule, these instructions refer to the timing of the examination; the fact that you should not start work until the signal and must stop work at a signal, etc. If there are any *special* instructions, such as a choice of questions to be answered, make sure that you note this instruction carefully.

2) When you are ready to start work on the examination, that is as soon as the signal has been given, read the instructions to each question booklet, underline any key words or phrases, such as *least, best, outline, describe* and the like. In this way you will tend to answer as requested rather than discover on reviewing your paper that you *listed without describing*, that you selected the *worst* choice rather than the *best* choice, etc.

3) If the examination is of the objective or multiple-choice type – that is, each question will also give a series of possible answers: A, B, C or D, and you are called upon to select the best answer and write the letter next to that answer on your answer paper – it is advisable to start answering each question in turn. There may be anywhere from 50 to 100 such questions in the three or four hours allotted and you can see how much time would be taken if you read through all the questions before beginning to answer any. Furthermore, if you come across a question or group of questions which you know would be difficult to answer, it would undoubtedly affect your handling of all the other questions.

4) If the examination is of the essay type and contains but a few questions, it is a moot point as to whether you should read all the questions before starting to answer any one. Of course, if you are given a choice – say five out of seven and the like – then it is essential to read all the questions so you can eliminate the two that are most difficult. If, however, you are asked to answer all the questions, there may be danger in trying to answer the easiest one first because you may find that you will spend too much time on it. The best technique is to answer the first question, then proceed to the second, etc.

5) Time your answers. Before the exam begins, write down the time it started, then add the time allowed for the examination and write down the time it must be completed, then divide the time available somewhat as follows:

- If 3-1/2 hours are allowed, that would be 210 minutes. If you have 80 objective-type questions, that would be an average of 2-1/2 minutes per question. Allow yourself no more than 2 minutes per question, or a total of 160 minutes, which will permit about 50 minutes to review.
- If for the time allotment of 210 minutes there are 7 essay questions to answer, that would average about 30 minutes a question. Give yourself only 25 minutes per question so that you have about 35 minutes to review.

6) The most important instruction is to *read each question* and make sure you know what is wanted. The second most important instruction is to *time yourself properly* so that you answer every question. The third most important instruction is to *answer every question*. Guess if you have to but include something for each question. Remember that you will receive no credit for a blank and will probably receive some credit if you write something in answer to an essay question. If you guess a letter – say "B" for a multiple-choice question – you may have guessed right. If you leave a blank as an answer to a multiple-choice question, the examiners may respect your feelings but it will not add a point to your score. Some exams may penalize you for wrong answers, so in such cases *only*, you may not want to guess unless you have some basis for your answer.

7) Suggestions
   a. Objective-type questions
      1. Examine the question booklet for proper sequence of pages and questions
      2. Read all instructions carefully
      3. Skip any question which seems too difficult; return to it after all other questions have been answered
      4. Apportion your time properly; do not spend too much time on any single question or group of questions
      5. Note and underline key words – *all, most, fewest, least, best, worst, same, opposite,* etc.
      6. Pay particular attention to negatives
      7. Note unusual option, e.g., unduly long, short, complex, different or similar in content to the body of the question
      8. Observe the use of "hedging" words – *probably, may, most likely,* etc.
      9. Make sure that your answer is put next to the same number as the question
      10. Do not second-guess unless you have good reason to believe the second answer is definitely more correct
      11. Cross out original answer if you decide another answer is more accurate; do not erase until you are ready to hand your paper in
      12. Answer all questions; guess unless instructed otherwise
      13. Leave time for review

   b. Essay questions
      1. Read each question carefully
      2. Determine exactly what is wanted. Underline key words or phrases.
      3. Decide on outline or paragraph answer

4. Include many different points and elements unless asked to develop any one or two points or elements
5. Show impartiality by giving pros and cons unless directed to select one side only
6. Make and write down any assumptions you find necessary to answer the questions
7. Watch your English, grammar, punctuation and choice of words
8. Time your answers; don't crowd material

8) Answering the essay question

Most essay questions can be answered by framing the specific response around several key words or ideas. Here are a few such key words or ideas:

M's: manpower, materials, methods, money, management
P's: purpose, program, policy, plan, procedure, practice, problems, pitfalls, personnel, public relations

a. Six basic steps in handling problems:
  1. Preliminary plan and background development
  2. Collect information, data and facts
  3. Analyze and interpret information, data and facts
  4. Analyze and develop solutions as well as make recommendations
  5. Prepare report and sell recommendations
  6. Install recommendations and follow up effectiveness

b. Pitfalls to avoid
  1. *Taking things for granted* – A statement of the situation does not necessarily imply that each of the elements is necessarily true; for example, a complaint may be invalid and biased so that all that can be taken for granted is that a complaint has been registered
  2. *Considering only one side of a situation* – Wherever possible, indicate several alternatives and then point out the reasons you selected the best one
  3. *Failing to indicate follow up* – Whenever your answer indicates action on your part, make certain that you will take proper follow-up action to see how successful your recommendations, procedures or actions turn out to be
  4. *Taking too long in answering any single question* – Remember to time your answers properly

IX. AFTER THE TEST

Scoring procedures differ in detail among civil service jurisdictions although the general principles are the same. Whether the papers are hand-scored or graded by machine we have described, they are nearly always graded by number. That is, the person who marks the paper knows only the number – never the name – of the applicant. Not until all the papers have been graded will they be matched with names. If other tests, such as training and experience or oral interview ratings have been given, scores will be combined. Different parts of the examination usually have different weights. For example, the written test might count 60 percent of the final grade, and a rating of training and experience 40 percent. In many jurisdictions, veterans will have a certain number of points added to their grades.

After the final grade has been determined, the names are placed in grade order and an eligible list is established. There are various methods for resolving ties between those who get the same final grade – probably the most common is to place first the name of the person whose application was received first. Job offers are made from the eligible list in the order the names appear on it. You will be notified of your grade and your rank as soon as all these computations have been made. This will be done as rapidly as possible.

People who are found to meet the requirements in the announcement are called "eligibles." Their names are put on a list of eligible candidates. An eligible's chances of getting a job depend on how high he stands on this list and how fast agencies are filling jobs from the list.

When a job is to be filled from a list of eligibles, the agency asks for the names of people on the list of eligibles for that job. When the civil service commission receives this request, it sends to the agency the names of the three people highest on this list. Or, if the job to be filled has specialized requirements, the office sends the agency the names of the top three persons who meet these requirements from the general list.

The appointing officer makes a choice from among the three people whose names were sent to him. If the selected person accepts the appointment, the names of the others are put back on the list to be considered for future openings.

That is the rule in hiring from all kinds of eligible lists, whether they are for typist, carpenter, chemist, or something else. For every vacancy, the appointing officer has his choice of any one of the top three eligibles on the list. This explains why the person whose name is on top of the list sometimes does not get an appointment when some of the persons lower on the list do. If the appointing officer chooses the second or third eligible, the No. 1 eligible does not get a job at once, but stays on the list until he is appointed or the list is terminated.

X. HOW TO PASS THE INTERVIEW TEST

The examination for which you applied requires an oral interview test. You have already taken the written test and you are now being called for the interview test – the final part of the formal examination.

You may think that it is not possible to prepare for an interview test and that there are no procedures to follow during an interview. Our purpose is to point out some things you can do in advance that will help you and some good rules to follow and pitfalls to avoid while you are being interviewed.

What is an interview supposed to test?

The written examination is designed to test the technical knowledge and competence of the candidate; the oral is designed to evaluate intangible qualities, not readily measured otherwise, and to establish a list showing the relative fitness of each candidate – as measured against his competitors – for the position sought. Scoring is not on the basis of "right" and "wrong," but on a sliding scale of values ranging from "not passable" to "outstanding." As a matter of fact, it is possible to achieve a relatively low score without a single "incorrect" answer because of evident weakness in the qualities being measured.

Occasionally, an examination may consist entirely of an oral test – either an individual or a group oral. In such cases, information is sought concerning the technical knowledges and abilities of the candidate, since there has been no written examination for this purpose. More commonly, however, an oral test is used to supplement a written examination.

Who conducts interviews?

The composition of oral boards varies among different jurisdictions. In nearly all, a representative of the personnel department serves as chairman. One of the members of the board may be a representative of the department in which the candidate would work. In some cases, "outside experts" are used, and, frequently, a businessman or some other representative of the general public is asked to serve. Labor and management or other special groups may be represented. The aim is to secure the services of experts in the appropriate field.

However the board is composed, it is a good idea (and not at all improper or unethical) to ascertain in advance of the interview who the members are and what groups they represent. When you are introduced to them, you will have some idea of their backgrounds and interests, and at least you will not stutter and stammer over their names.

What should be done before the interview?

While knowledge about the board members is useful and takes some of the surprise element out of the interview, there is other preparation which is more substantive. It *is* possible to prepare for an oral interview – in several ways:

1) Keep a copy of your application and review it carefully before the interview

This may be the only document before the oral board, and the starting point of the interview. Know what education and experience you have listed there, and the sequence and dates of all of it. Sometimes the board will ask you to review the highlights of your experience for them; you should not have to hem and haw doing it.

2) Study the class specification and the examination announcement

Usually, the oral board has one or both of these to guide them. The qualities, characteristics or knowledges required by the position sought are stated in these documents. They offer valuable clues as to the nature of the oral interview. For example, if the job involves supervisory responsibilities, the announcement will usually indicate that knowledge of modern supervisory methods and the qualifications of the candidate as a supervisor will be tested. If so, you can expect such questions, frequently in the form of a hypothetical situation which you are expected to solve. NEVER go into an oral without knowledge of the duties and responsibilities of the job you seek.

3) Think through each qualification required

Try to visualize the kind of questions you would ask if you were a board member. How well could you answer them? Try especially to appraise your own knowledge and background in each area, *measured against the job sought*, and identify any areas in which you are weak. Be critical and realistic – do not flatter yourself.

4) Do some general reading in areas in which you feel you may be weak
For example, if the job involves supervision and your past experience has NOT, some general reading in supervisory methods and practices, particularly in the field of human relations, might be useful. Do NOT study agency procedures or detailed manuals. The oral board will be testing your understanding and capacity, not your memory.

5) Get a good night's sleep and watch your general health and mental attitude
You will want a clear head at the interview. Take care of a cold or any other minor ailment, and of course, no hangovers.

What should be done on the day of the interview?
Now comes the day of the interview itself. Give yourself plenty of time to get there. Plan to arrive somewhat ahead of the scheduled time, particularly if your appointment is in the fore part of the day. If a previous candidate fails to appear, the board might be ready for you a bit early. By early afternoon an oral board is almost invariably behind schedule if there are many candidates, and you may have to wait. Take along a book or magazine to read, or your application to review, but leave any extraneous material in the waiting room when you go in for your interview. In any event, relax and compose yourself.

The matter of dress is important. The board is forming impressions about you – from your experience, your manners, your attitude, and your appearance. Give your personal appearance careful attention. Dress your best, but not your flashiest. Choose conservative, appropriate clothing, and be sure it is immaculate. This is a business interview, and your appearance should indicate that you regard it as such. Besides, being well groomed and properly dressed will help boost your confidence.

Sooner or later, someone will call your name and escort you into the interview room. *This is it.* From here on you are on your own. It is too late for any more preparation. But remember, you asked for this opportunity to prove your fitness, and you are here because your request was granted.

What happens when you go in?
The usual sequence of events will be as follows: The clerk (who is often the board stenographer) will introduce you to the chairman of the oral board, who will introduce you to the other members of the board. Acknowledge the introductions before you sit down. Do not be surprised if you find a microphone facing you or a stenotypist sitting by. Oral interviews are usually recorded in the event of an appeal or other review.

Usually the chairman of the board will open the interview by reviewing the highlights of your education and work experience from your application – primarily for the benefit of the other members of the board, as well as to get the material into the record. Do not interrupt or comment unless there is an error or significant misinterpretation; if that is the case, do not hesitate. But do not quibble about insignificant matters. Also, he will usually ask you some question about your education, experience or your present job – partly to get you to start talking and to establish the interviewing "rapport." He may start the actual questioning, or turn it over to one of the other members. Frequently, each member undertakes the questioning on a particular area, one in which he is perhaps most competent, so you can expect each member to participate in the examination. Because time is limited, you may also expect some rather abrupt switches in the direction the questioning takes, so do not be upset by it. Normally, a board member will not pursue a single line of questioning unless he discovers a particular strength or weakness.

After each member has participated, the chairman will usually ask whether any member has any further questions, then will ask you if you have anything you wish to add. Unless you are expecting this question, it may floor you. Worse, it may start you off on an extended, extemporaneous speech. The board is not usually seeking more information. The question is principally to offer you a last opportunity to present further qualifications or to indicate that you have nothing to add. So, if you feel that a significant qualification or characteristic has been overlooked, it is proper to point it out in a sentence or so. Do not compliment the board on the thoroughness of their examination – they have been sketchy, and you know it. If you wish, merely say, "No thank you, I have nothing further to add." This is a point where you can "talk yourself out" of a good impression or fail to present an important bit of information. Remember, *you close the interview yourself.*

The chairman will then say, "That is all, Mr. _____, thank you." Do not be startled; the interview is over, and quicker than you think. Thank him, gather your belongings and take your leave. Save your sigh of relief for the other side of the door.

How to put your best foot forward

Throughout this entire process, you may feel that the board individually and collectively is trying to pierce your defenses, seek out your hidden weaknesses and embarrass and confuse you. Actually, this is not true. They are obliged to make an appraisal of your qualifications for the job you are seeking, and they want to see you in your best light. Remember, they must interview all candidates and a non-cooperative candidate may become a failure in spite of their best efforts to bring out his qualifications. Here are 15 suggestions that will help you:

1) Be natural – Keep your attitude confident, not cocky

If you are not confident that you can do the job, do not expect the board to be. Do not apologize for your weaknesses, try to bring out your strong points. The board is interested in a positive, not negative, presentation. Cockiness will antagonize any board member and make him wonder if you are covering up a weakness by a false show of strength.

2) Get comfortable, but don't lounge or sprawl

Sit erectly but not stiffly. A careless posture may lead the board to conclude that you are careless in other things, or at least that you are not impressed by the importance of the occasion. Either conclusion is natural, even if incorrect. Do not fuss with your clothing, a pencil or an ashtray. Your hands may occasionally be useful to emphasize a point; do not let them become a point of distraction.

3) Do not wisecrack or make small talk

This is a serious situation, and your attitude should show that you consider it as such. Further, the time of the board is limited – they do not want to waste it, and neither should you.

4) Do not exaggerate your experience or abilities

In the first place, from information in the application or other interviews and sources, the board may know more about you than you think. Secondly, you probably will not get away with it. An experienced board is rather adept at spotting such a situation, so do not take the chance.

5) If you know a board member, do not make a point of it, yet do not hide it
   Certainly you are not fooling him, and probably not the other members of the board. Do not try to take advantage of your acquaintanceship – it will probably do you little good.

6) Do not dominate the interview
   Let the board do that. They will give you the clues – do not assume that you have to do all the talking. Realize that the board has a number of questions to ask you, and do not try to take up all the interview time by showing off your extensive knowledge of the answer to the first one.

7) Be attentive
   You only have 20 minutes or so, and you should keep your attention at its sharpest throughout. When a member is addressing a problem or question to you, give him your undivided attention. Address your reply principally to him, but do not exclude the other board members.

8) Do not interrupt
   A board member may be stating a problem for you to analyze. He will ask you a question when the time comes. Let him state the problem, and wait for the question.

9) Make sure you understand the question
   Do not try to answer until you are sure what the question is. If it is not clear, restate it in your own words or ask the board member to clarify it for you. However, do not haggle about minor elements.

10) Reply promptly but not hastily
   A common entry on oral board rating sheets is "candidate responded readily," or "candidate hesitated in replies." Respond as promptly and quickly as you can, but do not jump to a hasty, ill-considered answer.

11) Do not be peremptory in your answers
   A brief answer is proper – but do not fire your answer back. That is a losing game from your point of view. The board member can probably ask questions much faster than you can answer them.

12) Do not try to create the answer you think the board member wants
   He is interested in what kind of mind you have and how it works – not in playing games. Furthermore, he can usually spot this practice and will actually grade you down on it.

13) Do not switch sides in your reply merely to agree with a board member
   Frequently, a member will take a contrary position merely to draw you out and to see if you are willing and able to defend your point of view. Do not start a debate, yet do not surrender a good position. If a position is worth taking, it is worth defending.

14) Do not be afraid to admit an error in judgment if you are shown to be wrong
The board knows that you are forced to reply without any opportunity for careful consideration. Your answer may be demonstrably wrong. If so, admit it and get on with the interview.

15) Do not dwell at length on your present job
The opening question may relate to your present assignment. Answer the question but do not go into an extended discussion. You are being examined for a *new* job, not your present one. As a matter of fact, try to phrase ALL your answers in terms of the job for which you are being examined.

Basis of Rating

Probably you will forget most of these "do's" and "don'ts" when you walk into the oral interview room. Even remembering them all will not ensure you a passing grade. Perhaps you did not have the qualifications in the first place. But remembering them will help you to put your best foot forward, without treading on the toes of the board members.

Rumor and popular opinion to the contrary notwithstanding, an oral board wants you to make the best appearance possible. They know you are under pressure – but they also want to see how you respond to it as a guide to what your reaction would be under the pressures of the job you seek. They will be influenced by the degree of poise you display, the personal traits you show and the manner in which you respond.

ABOUT THIS BOOK

This book contains tests divided into Examination Sections. Go through each test, answering every question in the margin. At the end of each test look at the answer key and check your answers. On the ones you got wrong, look at the right answer choice and learn. Do not fill in the answers first. Do not memorize the questions and answers, but understand the answer and principles involved. On your test, the questions will likely be different from the samples. Questions are changed and new ones added. If you understand these past questions you should have success with any changes that arise. Tests may consist of several types of questions. We have additional books on each subject should more study be advisable or necessary for you. Finally, the more you study, the better prepared you will be. This book is intended to be the last thing you study before you walk into the examination room. Prior study of relevant texts is also recommended. NLC publishes some of these in our Fundamental Series. Knowledge and good sense are important factors in passing your exam. Good luck also helps. So now study this Passbook, absorb the material contained within and take that knowledge into the examination. Then do your best to pass that exam.

EXAMINATION SECTION

EXAMINATION SECTION
TEST 1

DIRECTIONS: Each question or incomplete statement is followed by several suggested answers or completions. Select the one that BEST answers the question or completes the statement. *PRINT THE LETTER OF THE CORRECT ANSWER IN THE SPACE AT THE RIGHT.*

1. A shop clerk is notified that only 75 bolts can be supplied by Vendor A. If this represents 12.5% of the total requisition, then how many bolts were *originally* ordered?

    A. 125   B. 600   C. 700   D. 900

2. An enclosed square-shaped storage area with sides of 16 feet each has a safe-load capacity of 250 pounds per square foot.
    The MAXIMUM evenly distributed weight that can be stored in this area is _____ lbs.

    A. 1,056   B. 4,000   C. 64,000   D. 102,400

3. A clerical employee has completed 70 progress reports the first week, 87 the second week, and 80 the third week. Assuming a 4-week month, how many progress reports must the clerk complete in the fourth week in order to attain an average of 85 progress reports per week for the month?

    A. 93   B. 103   C. 113   D. 133

4. On the first of the month, Shop X received a delivery of 150 gallons of lubricating oil. During the month, the following amounts of oil were used on lubricating work each week: 30 quarts, 36 quarts, 20 quarts, and 48 quarts. The amount of lubricating oil *remaining* at the end of the month was _____ gallons.

    A. 4   B. 33.5   C. 41.5   D. 116.5

5. For working a 35-hour week, Employee A earns a gross amount of $480.90. For each hour that Employee A works over 40 hours a week, he is entitled to 1 1/2 times his hourly wage rate.
    If Employee A worked 9 hours on Monday, 8 hours on Tuesday, 9 hours 30 minutes on Wednesday, 9 hours 15 minutes on Thursday, and 9 hours 15 minutes on Friday, what should his *gross* salary be for that week?

    A. $618.30   B. $632.04   C. $652.65   D. $687.00

6. An enclosed cube-shaped storage bay has dimensions of 12 feet by 12 feet by 12 feet. Standard procedure requires that there be at least 1 foot of space between the walls, the ceiling, and the stored items.
    What is the MAXIMUM number of cube-shaped boxes with length, width, and height of 1 foot each that can be stored on 1-foot high pallets in this bay?

    A. 1,000   B. 1,331   C. 1,452   D. 1,728

7. Assume that two ceilings are to be painted. One ceiling measures 30 feet by 15 feet and the second 45 feet by 60 feet.
    If one quart of paint will cover 60 square feet of ceiling, *approximately* how much paint will be required to paint the two ceilings? _____ gallons.

A. 6 B. 10 C. 13 D. 18

8. In last year's budget, $7,500 was spent for office supplies. Of this amount, 60% was spent for paper supplies. If the price of paper has risen 20% over last year's price, then the amount that will be spent this year on paper supplies, assuming the same quantity will be purchased, will be

8.___

A. $3,600 B. $5,200 C. $5,400 D. $6,000

Questions 9-13.

DIRECTIONS: Questions 9 through 13 are to be answered on the basis of the following information.

A certain shop keeps an informational card file on all suppliers and merchandise. On each card is the supplier's name, the contrast number for the merchandise he supplies, and a delivery date for the merchandise. In this filing system, the supplier's name is filed alphabetically, the contract number for the merchandise is filed numerically, and the delivery date is filed chronologically.

In Questions 9 through 13, there are five notations numbered 1 through 5 shown in Column I. Each notation is made up of a supplier's name, a contract number, and a date which is to be filed according to the following rules:

First: File in alphabetical order
Second: When two or more notations have the same supplier, file according to the contract number in numerical order beginning with the lowest number
Third: When two or more notations have the same supplier and contract number, file according to the date beginning with the earliest date.

In Column II, the numbers 1 through 5 are arranged in four ways to show four different orders in which the merchandise information might be filed. Pick the answer (A, B, C, or D) in Column II in which the notations are arranged according to the above filing rules.

SAMPLE QUESTION:

COLUMN I	COLUMN II
1. Cluney (4865) 6/17/05	A. 2, 3, 4, 1, 5
2. Roster (2466) 5/10/04	B. 2, 5, 1, 3, 4
3. Altool (7114) 10/15/05	C. 3, 2, 1, 4, 5
4. Cluney (5276) 12/18/04	D. 3, 5, 1, 4, 2
5. Cluney (4865) 4/8/05	

The CORRECT way to file the cards is:

3. Altool (7114) 10/15/05
5. Cluney (4865) 4/8/05
1. Cluney (4865) 6/17/05
4. Cluney (5276) 12/18/04
2. Roster (2466) 5/10/04

Since the correct filing order is 3, 5, 1, 4, 2, the answer to the sample question is D.

COLUMN I		COLUMN II	
9.	1. Warren (96063) 3/30/06 2. Moore (21237) 9/4/07 3. Newman (10050) 12/12/06 4. Downs (81251) 1/2/06 5. Oliver (60145) 6/30/07	A. 2, 4, 3, 5, 1 B. 2, 3, 5, 4, 1 C. 4, 5, 2, 3, 1 D. 4, 2, 3, 5, 1	9.____
10.	1. Henry (40552) 7/6/07 2. Boyd (91251) 9/1/06 3. George (8196) 12/12/06 4. George (31096) 1/12/07 5. West (6109) 8/9/06	A. 5, 4, 3, 1, 2 B. 2, 3, 4, 1, 5 C. 2, 4, 3, 1, 5 D. 5, 2, 3, 1, 4	10.____
11.	1. Salba (4670) 9/7/06 2. Salba (51219) 3/1/06 3. Crete (81562) 7/1/07 4. Salba (51219) 1/11/07 5. Texi (31549) 1/25/06	A. 5, 3, 1, 2, 4 B. 3, 1, 2, 4, 5 C. 3, 5, 4, 2, 1 D. 5, 3, 4, 2, 1	11.____
12.	1. Crayone (87105) 6/10/07 2. Shamba (49210) 1/5/06 3. Valiant (3152) 5/1/07 4. Valiant (3152) 1/9/07 5. Poro (59613) 7/1/06	A. 1, 2, 5, 3, 4 B. 1, 5, 2, 3, 4 C. 1, 5, 3, 4, 2 D. 1, 5, 2, 4, 3	12.____
13.	1. Mackie (42169) 12/20/06 2. Lebo (5198) 9/12/05 3. Drummon (99631) 9/9/07 4. Lebo (15311) 1/25/05 5. Harvin (81765) 6/2/06	A. 3, 2, 1, 5, 4 B. 3, 2, 4, 5, 1 C. 3, 5, 2, 4, 1 D. 3, 5, 4, 2, 1	13.____

Questions 14-18.

DIRECTIONS: Questions 14 through 18 are to be answered on the basis of the following information.

In order to make sure stock is properly located, incoming units are stored as follows:

Stock Numbers	Bin Numbers
00100 - 39999	D30, L44
40000 - 69999	I4L, D38
70000 - 99999	41L, 80D
100000 and over	614, 83D

Using the above table, choose the answer (A, B, C, or D) which lists the correct bin number for the stock number given.

14. 17243

    A. 41L   B. 83D   C. I4L   D. D30

15. 9219

    A. D38   B. L44   C. 614   D. 41L

16. 90125

    A. 41L   B. 614   C. D38   D. D30

17. 10001

    A. L44   B. D38   C. SOD   D. 83D

18. 200100

    A. 41L   B. I4L   C. 83D   D. D30

19. A supervisor believes that the current filing systems used in his office are not efficient. When his superior goes on vacation, he intends to change all the filing procedures. For a supervisor to undertake this move without his superior's knowledge would GENERALLY be considered

    A. *advisable;* it shows that he has initiative
    B. *inadvisable;* the current filing systems are probably the best
    C. *advisable;* the result will be an increase in productivity
    D. *inadvisable;* the supervisor should be informed of any intended changes

20. Assume that you have been assigned the task of handling all telephone calls at a sanitation garage. After a recent snowstorm, your supervisor informed you that all available personnel have been assigned to snow removal duties. However, you have been receiving numerous telephone calls from the public in regard to unshoveled streets and intersections.
    In handling these calls, it is generally considered good policy by the department to

    A. indicate to the callers that the department is clearing streets off as quickly as possible
    B. tell the callers there is nothing that can be done
    C. tell the callers that they are tying up departmental telephones with needless complaints
    D. promise the callers that streets will be cleared by the evening

KEY (CORRECT ANSWERS)

1.	B	11.	B
2.	C	12.	D
3.	B	13.	C
4.	D	14.	D
5.	C	15.	B
6.	A	16.	A
7.	C	17.	A
8.	C	18.	C
9.	D	19.	D
10.	B	20.	A

TEST 2

DIRECTIONS: Each question or incomplete statement is followed by several suggested answers or completions. Select the one that BEST answers the question or completes the statement. *PRINT THE LETTER OF TEE CORRECT ANSWER IN THE SPACE AT THE RIGHT.*

Questions 1-10.

DIRECTIONS: Questions 1 through 10 are to be answered on the basis of the following information.

A code number for any item is obtained by combining the date of delivery, number of units received, and number of units used.

The first two digits represent the day of the month, the third and fourth digits represent the month, and the fifth and sixth digits represent the year.

The number following the letter R represents the number of units received and the number following the letter U represents the number of units used.

For example, the code number 120673-R5690-U1001 indicates that a delivery of 5,690 units was made on June 12, of which 1,001 units were used.

Using the chart below, answer Questions 1 through 6 by choosing the letter (A, B, C, or D) in which the supplier and stock number correspond to the code number given.

Supplier	Stock Number	Number of Units Received	Delivery Date	Number of Units Used
Stony	38390	8300	May 11	3800
Stoney	39803	1780	September 15	1703
Nievo	21220	5527	October 10	5007
Nieve	38903	1733	August 5	1703
Monte	39213	5527	October 10	5007
Stony	38890	3308	December 9	3300
Stony	83930	3880	September 12	380
Nevo	47101	485	June 11	231
Nievo	12122	5725	May 11	5201
Neve	47101	9721	August 15	8207
Nievo	21120	2275	January 7	2175
Rosa	41210	3821	March 3	2710
Stony	38890	3308	September 12	3300
Dinal	54921	1711	April 2	1117
Stony	33890	8038	March 5	3300
Dinal	54721	1171	March 2	717
Claridge	81927	3308	April 5	3088
Nievo	21122	4878	June 7	3492
Haley	39670	8300	December 23	5300

1. Code No. 120972-R3308-U3300   1._____

    A. Nievo - 12122   B. Stony - 83930
    C. Nievo - 21220   D. Stony - 38890

6

2. Code No. 101072-R5527-U5007

    A. Nievo - 21220
    B. Haley - 39670
    C. Monte - 39213
    D. Claridge - 81927

3. Code No. 101073-R5527-U5007

    A. Nievo - 21220
    B. Monte - 39213
    C. Nievo - 12122
    D. Nievo - 21120

4. Code No. 110573-R5725-U5201

    A. Nievo - 12122
    B. Nievo - 21220
    C. Haley - 39670
    D. Stony - 38390

5. Code No. 070172-R2275-U2175

    A. Stony - 33890
    B. Stony - 83930
    C. Stony - 38390
    D. Nievo - 21120

6. Code No. 120972-R3880-U380

    A. Stony - 83930
    B. Stony - 38890
    C. Stony - 33890
    D. Monte - 39213

Using the same chart, answer Questions 7 through 10, choosing the letter (A, B, C, or D) in which the code number corresponds to the supplier and stock number given.

7. Nieve - 38903

    A. 951973-R1733-U1703
    B. 080572-R1733-U1703
    C. 080573-R1733-U1703
    D. 050873-R1733-U1703

8. Nevo - 47101

    A. 081573-R9721-U8207
    B. 091573-R9721-U8207]
    C. 110672-R485-U231
    D. 061172-R485-U231

9. Dinal - 54921

    A. 020473-R1711-U1117
    B. 030272-R1171-U717
    C. 020372-R1171-U717
    D. 421973-R1711-U1117

10. Nievo - 21122

    A. 070672-R4878-U3492
    B. 060772-R4878-U349
    C. 761972-R4878-U3492
    D. 060772-R4878-U3492

11. A citizen who has called the office at which you are working has started yelling on the telephone. He is annoyed because he has been switched from office to office and still has not reached the proper party.
    Of the following, the BEST practice to follow is to

    A. hang up on this individual since he is obviously a troublemaker
    B. yell back at him for being so childish
    C. tell him that you have heard that complaint before
    D. try to calm this person and help him reach the proper party

12. Which of the following is the MOST likely result of employees publicly criticizing the activities of their agency?
The

   A. employees will be terminated for the good of the agency
   B. public's respect for the agency may decrease
   C. productive members of the agency may resign
   D. agency may sue these employees for libel

13. It is essential for city employees who deal with the public to provide service as promptly and completely as possible.
Letters from the public lodging complaints regarding poor service should GENERALLY be handled by

   A. answering them as soon as possible according to agency procedures
   B. ignoring them, since only troublemakers usually write such letters
   C. returning them, since the city government does not respond to public complaints
   D. acknowledging them with no further action necessary

14. While checking the work of a clerk who is under your supervision, you notice that he has made the same mistake a number of times.
In order to help prevent this clerk from making the same mistake again, it would be BEST for you to take which of the following courses of action?

   A. Correct the errors yourself and not mention it to the clerk
   B. Provide training for the clerk
   C. Reprimand the clerk for the mistakes made
   D. Remind the clerk of the errors he has previously made

15. A community resident calls the sanitation garage in which you are working to inquire about the days in which old furniture can be put on the street for collection. Although your unit is responsible for these collections, you do not have this information and there is nobody in the office to assist you.
Of the following, it would be MOST advisable to

   A. tell the citizen to call back in an hour
   B. get the citizen's telephone number and inform him that you will call back when you get the information
   C. switch the call to another unit and let them get the information
   D. put the caller on hold and try to find someone that has the answer

16. As a supervisor, you have been given the responsibility of maintaining attendance records for your garage. A co-worker, who has been late a number of times, has asked you to overlook his recent lateness since it involves only ten minutes. He has been warned previously for lateness and will receive some kind of disciplinary action because of this recent lateness, for you to overlook the lateness would be

   A. *advisable;* it involves only a matter of ten minutes
   B. *inadvisable;* this employee should have to suffer the consequences of his actions
   C. *advisable;* morale in the unit will improve
   D. *inadvisable;* employee lateness should never be excused

17. When a supervisor answers incoming telephone calls, it is important for him to FIRST   17._____

    A. identify himself and/or his office
    B. ask the caller to state the reason for the call
    C. ask the caller the nature of the call
    D. ask the caller to identify himself

18. It appears to you that the current mail distribution procedures are inefficient.   18._____
    For you to make a suggestion to your supervisor for the implementation of new procedures, would be

    A. *advisable;* if the supervisor thinks your ideas are worthwhile;they may be implemented
    B. *inadvisable;* supervisors generally are not interested in changing procedures
    C. *advisable;* new procedures generally provide better results than old procedures
    D. *inadvisable;* only methods analysts should suggest changes in procedures

19. As a supervisor, you direct the work of two clerks. Recently, you discovered that one of   19._____
    the two clerks generally loafs around on Friday afternoons. This past Friday, you saw this particular employee standing around conversing with several employees. At that point, you severely reprimanded this employee in the presence of the other employees.
    For you to have reprimanded this employee in such a fashion was

    A. *advisable;* this employee *had it coming*
    B. *inadvisable;* you should have spoken to him privately
    C. *advisable;* this reprimand also served as a warning to the others
    D. *inadvisable;* employees should not be reprimanded

20. As a supervisor, you have been assigned to maintain garage supplies. Recently, a co-   20._____
    worker requested a quantity of nails and screws for use in his home. Since this involves only a small amount of supplies, he felt it would not be wrong to make such a request.
    In this case, it would be ADVISABLE for you to

    A. give the co-worker the supplies
    B. remind the co-worker that city supplies are only for city use
    C. notify the investigation department in regard to this employee
    D. forget the incident

KEY (CORRECT ANSWERS)

1.	D	11.	D
2.	C	12.	B
3.	A	13.	A
4.	A	14.	B
5.	D	15.	B
6.	A	16.	B
7.	D	17.	A
8.	C	18.	A
9.	A	19.	B
10.	A	20.	B

EXAMINATION SECTION
TEST 1

DIRECTIONS: Each question or incomplete statement is followed by several suggested answers or completions. Select the one that BEST answers the question or completes the statement. *PRINT THE LETTER OF THE CORRECT ANSWER IN THE SPACE AT THE RIGHT.*

1. The MOST effective way for you to inform your subordinates of a new storage procedure that is to be instituted within the next two months is to

    A. distribute printed sheets describing the new procedure to all those involved
    B. assign your most capable assistant stockman to explain the new procedure to the others
    C. conduct a meeting with all your men and explain the new procedure to them
    D. begin practicing the new procedure immediately

    1.____

2. The LEAST effective method of training a new inexperienced assistant stockman in storage techniques used in your section is to

    A. have him observe an experienced assistant stockman at work
    B. allow him to perform some work under your watchful guidance
    C. have another employee explain the procedures to him
    D. assign a job to him where he can work alone and learn by himself

    2.____

3. If totally new procedures in your stockroom are going to be started very shortly, the BEST method of training the assistant stockmen in their use is to

    A. hold one long training session where all aspects of the new procedures are discussed
    B. conduct short training sessions over a span of time with a few topics at each session
    C. conduct individual training sessions for each of the assistant stockmen in your unit
    D. hold training sessions only for the less inexperienced assistant stockmen in your unit

    3.____

4. If an assistant stockman approaches you to discuss a complicated problem about a shipment that will be coming in next week and you find yourself very busy, the BEST thing for you to do is to tell him

    A. to stop worrying since you will take care of things
    B. that you will call him in, as soon as possible, to explain the procedures to him
    C. that he must describe his problem very briefly as your time is limited
    D. to state the problem in writing so you can study it later

    4.____

5. If, during a meeting, an assistant stockman asks you a question that you cannot answer, the BEST way to handle this situation is to

    A. explain that you do not know the answer but you will get the information as soon as possible
    B. tell the assistant stockman to ask someone else in the department
    C. attempt to answer the question with whatever knowledge you have on the subject
    D. tell the assistant stockman to save his question for some future date

    5.____

6. Two of your assistant stockmen want to take off next Friday. You know that a large shipment is expected that day and one of them must be present. The BEST thing to do is to

   A. suggest that they first try to decide between themselves who is to work
   B. ask your own superior who should be required to work that day
   C. explain to the men that they should both come into work next Friday to avoid problems of favoritism
   D. tell them that the one with the most recent absence should come in

7. One of your assistant stockmen has been consistently late for work for more than a week. The FIRST thing you should do is

   A. take disciplinary action against him
   B. ask him personally about the reason for his lateness
   C. assign him to a section that is busy mainly in the afternoon
   D. ask your supervisor for advice on the situation

8. The CORRECT way to lift a heavy box is to keep your feet

   A. close together, crouch close to the load, and keep your back straight as you rise
   B. apart, crouch an arm's length away from the load, and keep your back arched as you rise
   C. close together, crouch close to the load, and keep your back arched as you rise
   D. apart, crouch close to the load, and keep your back straight as you rise

9. When two or more men are carrying a heavy box, the possibility of an accident is MOST likely if the men carrying the box

   A. are all of similar size and physique
   B. do not coordinate their movement in avoiding obstacles in their path
   C. use predetermined signals to control lifting and carrying motions
   D. do not shift too much weight onto any one of them

10. If your section is criticized for making an error, you should FIRST

    A. blame the employee you feel is responsible
    B. analyze the reasons why the error was made in your section
    C. assign men to work overtime to correct the error
    D. avoid favoritism by blaming all the employees for poor work habits

11. If you find that several of your assistant stockmen are making mistakes in new procedures recently taught to them, you should

    A. train other assistant stockmen who show more initiative in their work
    B. write to your superior requesting a change back to the old procedures
    C. hold another training session for these men to help them recall the details of the new procedures
    D. correct the mistakes yourself since you are responsible for the actions of your employees

12. A stockman can encourage cooperation in all of the following ways EXCEPT by

    A. disregarding the good suggestions that his subordinates make
    B. recognizing his employees as distinct individuals

C. making it possible for subordinates to get out their production on time
D. giving his subordinates credit due them for the work they do

13. To make a fair and realistic judgment of how well an employee under your supervision does his job, you should

    A. compare the performance of this employee with that of your best employee
    B. compare the performance of this employee with the performance level expected for this position
    C. base your judgment mainly on the lateness record of the employee
    D. base your judgment mainly on the cooperation you get from the employee

14. One of your subordinates approaches you with a good suggestion for work improvement that he wants to submit to the employees' suggestion program. The BEST action you should take is to

    A. help him refine the suggestion and have him submit it officially to the program
    B. first show the suggestion to your fellow workers to see if it has been implemented in the past
    C. call a general staff meeting to get the other employees' opinion of this suggestion
    D. explain that the suggestion would get more recognition if it were submitted by a supervisory staff member

15. One assistant stockman in your unit seems intelligent and is well educated. Although he is a fast worker, he makes many errors. However, he asks you to assign more responsible tasks to him.
    The BEST approach in this situation is for you to

    A. tell him to speak to your superior
    B. grant his request for more responsible work
    C. tell him that he works fast, but more accuracy is required before he can be given more responsibility
    D. tell him that he should speak to the personnel officer if he is unsatisfied with his present duties

16. If you are approached privately by an assistant stockman who has a problem on the job, you should do all of the following EXCEPT

    A. pay strict attention to what he is saying
    B. maintain a running mental summary of what his basic message is
    C. look away from him while he is speaking to you in order to avoid embarrassing him
    D. ask him questions about anything that is not clear to you

17. When a stockman is conducting a meeting with his assistant stockmen, he should do all of the following EXCEPT

    A. use plain and simple words
    B. talk at a moderately slow speed
    C. use voice inflections and gestures to emphasize key points
    D. speak in long detailed sentences

18. If an assistant stockman receives a burn but his skin does not blister, you should FIRST 18._____

   A. apply cold water to the burn
   B. write out the accident report
   C. send the man home to rest
   D. assign the man to a less strenuous job for the rest of the day

19. Two of your assistant stockmen are working together on a job. They do not get along with each other and constantly argue, disturbing the other men. The MOST effective action to take would be to 19._____

   A. transfer both employees to other sections
   B. speak to both men in private to find out what is wrong
   C. discipline the man who you think is causing the trouble
   D. assign both men to perform the least desirable duties as punishment

20. A package marked COMBUSTIBLE should be handled cautiously because it may result in a(n) 20._____

   A. bad burn
   B. electric shock
   C. severe headache
   D. chronic eye irritation

KEY (CORRECT ANSWERS)

1.	C	11.	C
2.	D	12.	A
3.	B	13.	B
4.	B	14.	A
5.	A	15.	C
6.	A	16.	C
7.	B	17.	D
8.	D	18.	A
9.	B	19.	B
10.	B	20.	A

TEST 2

DIRECTIONS: Each question or incomplete statement is followed by several suggested answers or completions. Select the one that BEST answers the question or completes the statement. *PRINT THE LETTER OF THE CORRECT ANSWER IN THE SPACE AT THE RIGHT.*

Questions 1-4.

DIRECTIONS: Questions 1 through 4 are to be answered on the basis of the following alphabetical rules.

RULES FOR ALPHABETICAL FILING

Names of Individuals

The names of individuals are filed in strict alphabetical order, first according to the last name, then according to first name or initial, and finally according to middle name or initial. For example: George Allen precedes Edward Bell and Leonard Reston precedes Lucille Reston.

When last names are the same, for example, A. Green and Agnes Green, the one with the initial comes before the one with the name written out when the first initials are identical.

Prefixes such as De, O', Mac, Mc, and Van are filed as written and are treated as part of the names to which they are connected. For example: Gladys McTeaque is filed before Frances Meadows.

1. If the following four names were put into an alphabetical list, what would the FIRST name on the list be?

    A. Wm. C. Paul
    B. W. Paul
    C. Alice Paul
    D. Alyce Paul

    1.____

2. If the following four names were put into an alphabetical list, what would the THIRD name on the list be?

    A. I. MacCarthy
    B. Irene MacKarthy
    C. Ida McCaren
    D. I. A. McCarthy

    2.____

3. If the following four names were put into an alphabetical list, what would the SECOND name on the list be?

    A. John Gilhooley
    B. Ramon Gonzalez
    C. Gerald Gilholy
    D. Samuel Gilvechhio

    3.____

4. If the following four names were put into an alphabetical list, what would the FOURTH name on the list be?

    A. Michael Edwinn
    B. James Edwards
    C. Mary Edwin
    D. Carlo Edwards

    4.____

5. An employee in the stockroom suggests to his supervisor that records involving stock transactions should not be numerically filed. The employee suggested that the records simply be stored in a cabinet after processing. Whenever a record is needed, someone can go through the records in the cabinet and pick the one they need. Such a suggestion is

   A. *good,* because it will save time since the stock records do not have to be filed
   B. *bad,* because records that are filed are often mis-filed and this procedure eliminates the need for filing
   C. *bad,* because many file clerks will have less work to do with the new procedures
   D. *bad,* because filed records can be found quicker than records that are not filed

6. A stockman who is working in a warehouse is given the responsibility for telephoning vendors when the vendors are late in sending the balance of a partial delivery.
   It has been decided that for most stock items the vendors are to be given ten working days in which to deliver the balance of stock items. Since there is a large volume of stock deliveries, the stockman has decided to set up a filing system so that he is reminded of when to call the vendors.
   It would be BEST to set up such a filing system on the basis of

   A. name of the vendor who is to send the stock
   B. commodity code of the stock item
   C. date that the telephone call should be made
   D. date that the purchase order was processed

Questions 7-10.

DIRECTIONS: Questions 7 through 10 each contain five numbers that should be arranged in numerical order. The number with the lowest numerical value should be first and the number with the highest numerical value should be last.

Pick that option which indicates the CORRECT order of the numbers.
Examples: A. 9, 18, 14, 15, 27
           B. 9, 14, 15, 18, 27
           C. 14, 15, 18, 27, 9
           D. 9, 14, 15, 27, 18
The correct answer is B, which indicates the proper arrangement of the five numbers.

7. A. 20573, 20753, 20738, 20837, 20098
   B. 20098, 20753, 20573, 20738, 20837
   C. 20098, 20573, 20753, 20837, 20738
   D. 20098, 20573, 20738, 20753, 20837

8. A. 113492, 113429, 111314, 113114, 131413
   B. 111314, 113114, 113429, 113492, 131413
   C. 111314, 113429, 113492, 113114, 131413
   D. 111314, 113114, 131413, 113429, 113492

9. A. 1029763, 1030421, 1034581, 1036928, 1067391
    B. 1030421, 1029763, 1034681, 1067391, 1036928
    C. 1030421, 1035681, 1036928, 1067391, 1029763
    D. 1029763, 1039421, 1035681, 1067391, 1036928

10. A. 1112315, 1112326, 1112337, 1112349, 1112306
    B. 1112306, 1112315, 1112337, 1112326, 1112349
    C. 1112306, 1112315, 1112326, 1112337, 1112349
    D. 1112306, 1112326, 1112315, 1112337, 1112349

Questions 11-20.

DIRECTIONS: Each of Questions 11 through 20 presents a stock item followed by four general classification groups. For each question, choose the general classification group in which the given item is MOST likely to be found.

11. *Filing cabinets* may BEST be classified under

    A. laboratory apparatus
    B. furniture, furnishings, kitchen equipment, supplies, and utensils
    C. metals
    D. plumbers, steamfitters, and machinists supplies

12. *Fiber board* may BEST be classified under

    A. hardware (not otherwise classified)
    B. miscellaneous
    C. materials of construction
    D. office supplies and stationery

13. *Rhubarb* may BEST be classified under

    A. forage
    B. hose and belting
    C. hospital supplies and surgical instruments
    D. goods and food products

14. *Cotton twine* can BEST be classified under

    A. clothing and wearing apparel
    B. cordage and rope
    C. materials of construction
    D. office supplies and stationery

15. *Mop handles* may BEST be classified under

    A. cleaning compounds and insecticides
    B. tools and implements
    C. cleaning equipment
    D. miscellaneous

16. *Pecan lumber* may BEST be classified under

   A. food and food products
   B. materials of construction
   C. seeds, plants, trees, and botanical supplies
   D. tools and implements

17. *Putty* may BEST be classified under

   A. paints, oils, varnishes, painters supplies
   B. materials of construction
   C. pipes, valves, and pipe fittings
   D. oils, greases, and lubricants

18. *Analytical filter paper* may BEST be classified under

   A. laboratory apparatus and supplies
   B. drugs and chemicals
   C. photographic equipment
   D. office supplies and stationery

19. *Work aprons* may BEST be classified under

   A. laboratory apparatus
   B. cleaning equipment
   C. dry goods and notions
   D. hospital and surgical instruments

20. *Fowl* may BEST be classified under

   A. cleaning compounds and insecticides
   B. drugs and chemicals
   C. foods and food products
   D. livestock and laboratory animals

Questions 21-25.

DIRECTIONS: Questions 21 through 25 contain incomplete requisitions. These requisitions cannot be filled because essential information is missing. You are to select the term which will CORRECTLY complete the incomplete requisition. (Note that commodity number and quantity are not to be considered.

21. Pencil, black lead, #2, general office use, _____

   A. wood   B. very soft
   C. 7 1/2 inches   D. with eraser

22. Screw, wood, flat head, 1/4 inch, #3, 100 per package, _____

   A. sheet metal   B. galvanized
   C. brass   D. bright

23. Ladders, extension, 2 sections, metal, _____

   A. aluminum   B. 30 feet
   C. 45 pounds   D. silver (color)

24. Stoppers, rubber, solid, nickel-plated brass ring, 1-inch diameter, _____   24.____
    A. white   B. bathtub   C. 1 ounce   D. round

25. Thermometer, oven, enamel, _____   25.____
    A. mercury   B. kelvin   C. 100/600F   D. 8 inch

KEY (CORRECT ANSWERS)

1.	C	11.	B
2.	C	12.	C
3.	A	13.	D
4.	A	14.	B
5.	D	15.	C
6.	C	16.	B
7.	D	17.	A
8.	B	18.	A
9.	A	19.	C
10.	C	20.	C

21. D
22. C
23. B
24. A
25. C

EXAMINATION SECTION
TEST 1

DIRECTIONS: Each question or incomplete statement is followed by several suggested answers or completions. Select the one that BEST answers the question or completes the statement. *PRINT THE LETTER OF THE CORRECT ANSWER IN THE SPACE AT THE RIGHT.*

1. One of the results of understocking is that

   A. more money is tied up in stock
   B. stock must be ordered more frequently
   C. there is greater likelihood of obsolescence
   D. there is uneven distribution of materials in storage

2. Assume that your re-order point is obtained by multiplying the monthly rate of consumption by the lead time (in months) and adding the minimum balance. For a particular item, the re-order point is established at 200 units.
   If the lead time is 2 months and the minimum balance is 100, then the average monthly rate of consumption is

   A. 50   B. 100   C. 150   D. 200

3. If a certain item has shown no activity for two years, the MOST advisable action to take FIRST is to

   A. attempt to dispose of the item through salvage
   B. contact the using agencies or individuals to determine whether they can use the item
   C. contact the vendor to determine whether the item can be traded in
   D. write it off on the inventory control card

4. The MOST important information on an inventory control card is that which gives the _____ of the item.

   A. identity   B. location
   C. rate of consumption D. vendor

5. A space 5 1/4 feet wide and 2 1/3 feet long has an area measuring MOST NEARLY _____ square feet.

   A. 9   B. 10   C. 11   D. 12

6. One man is able to load two 2 1/2-ton trucks in one hour. To load ten such trucks, it will take ten men _____ hour(s).

   A. 1/2   B. 1   C. 2   D. 2 1/2

7. If the average height of the stacks in your section of the storehouse is 10 feet, the area which will be occupied by 56,000 cubic feet of supplies is MOST likely to be

   A. 70' x 80'   B. 60' x 90'   C. 50' x 60'   D. 560' x 100'

8. The number of cartons, each measuring two cubic feet, which can fit into a space which is 100 square feet in area and is 8 feet high is MOST NEARLY

   A. 50   B. 200   C. 400   D. 800

9. When the floor area measures 200 feet by 200 feet and the maximum weight it can hold is 4,000 tons, then the safe floor load is _____ pounds per square foot.

   A. 20   B. 160   C. 200   D. 400

10. A carton 1' x 1' x 3' measures _____ cubic yards.

    A. 1/3   B. 1/9   C. 3   D. 9

11. You have received six cartons, each containing sixty boxes of staples, priced at $36.00 per carton.
    The price per box is

    A. $.10   B. $.60   C. $3.60   D. $6.00

12. The amount of space, in cubic feet, required to store 100 boxes each measuring 24" x 12" x 6" is MOST NEARLY

    A. 10   B. 100   C. 168   D. 1008

13. Assume that it takes an average of two man-hours to stack 1 ton of certain supplies. In order to stack 30 tons, the number of men required to complete the job in ten hours is

    A. 6   B. 10   C. 15   D. 30

14. An area measures 20 feet by 22 1/2 feet. The floor load is 100 pounds per square foot. The total weight that can be stored in this area is MOST NEARLY _____ pounds.

    A. 450   B. 9,000   C. 22,500   D. 45,000

15. The price of a certain type of linoleum is $.20 per square foot.
    The total cost of four pieces of 9' x 12' linoleum is MOST NEARLY

    A. $21   B. $80   C. $86   D. $432

16. The number of board feet in a piece of lumber measuring 2 inches thick by 2 feet wide by 12 feet long is

    A. 12   B. 16   C. 24   D. 48

17. If 39 3/8 ounces of a certain commodity are on hand and two requisitions are filled, one for 9 1/2 and one for 9 5/6 ounces, the number of ounces remaining are

    A. 18 2/3   B. 19 1/3   C. 20 1/24   D. 20 3/4

18. In order to fill 96 bottles containing 3 fluid ounces each, the number of pints which would be needed is

    A. 9   B. 18   C. 32   D. 36

19. If a section of a storeroom measures 29 feet 4 inches by 18 feet 3 inches, the total area is MOST NEARLY _____ square feet.

    A. 523   B. 524   C. 535   D. 537

3 (#1)

20. A discount of 1% is given on all purchases of over 100 brushes. An additional discount of 1% is given on all purchases of over 500 brushes.
If 600 brushes are purchased at a list price of $2.07 each, the total cost is MOST NEARLY

    A. $1217   B. $1228   C. $1230   D. $2484

20.____

21. The following items are purchased: 30 locksets at $15.00 per dozen, and 10 gross of stove bolts at 1 1/2 cents each bolt.
The total cost is MOST NEARLY

    A. $60   B. $180   C. $255   D. $470

21.____

22. The cost of one dozen pieces of screening, each measuring 4'6" by 5', at $.10 per square foot, is

    A. $22.50   B. $25.00   C. $27.00   D. $27.60

22.____

23. The amount of turpentine on hand is 39 gallons. One requisition is filled for 3 1/2 gallons, three additional requisitions are filled for 3 quarts each, and six requisitions are filled for 1 pint each.
The quantity of turpentine remaining after all these requisitions have been filled is

    A. 32 gal.   B. 32 gal. 1 qt.
    C. 32 gal. 2 qts.   D. 32 gal. 3 qts.

23.____

24. A shelf is 30" wide and 20" deep. The shelf is filled solid with 500 boxes, each measuring 2" x 3" x 5". The distance from the shelf to the top of the stacked boxes is

    A. 10"   B. 25"   C. 50"   D. 60"

24.____

25. In order to check on a shipment of 1000 articles, a sampling of 100 articles was carefully inspected.
Of the sample, one article was wholly defective and 4 more were partly defective.
On this basis, the percentage of completely acceptable articles in the original shipment is probably MOST NEARLY

    A. 5%   B. 10%   C. 95%   D. 100%

25.____

26. The one of the following which is NOT the name of a type of screwdriver is

    A. cabinet   B. flat-nose
    C. knife handle   D. spiral ratchet

26.____

27. Pupil Dental Record forms are likely to be used in GREATEST quantities by the

    A. Board of Education   B. Department of Health
    C. Department of Hospitals   D. Department of Social Service

27.____

28. Crepe paper is likely to be requisitioned MOST frequently by the

    A. Board of Education   B. Department of Public Events
    C. Housing Authority   D. Transit Authority

28.____

29. Scalpels are likely to be requisitioned MOST frequently by the Department of

    A. Correction   B. Health
    C. Hospitals   D. Parks

30. Pruners are likely to be requisitioned MOST frequently by the

    A. Department of Parks   B. Department of Sanitation
    C. Reference Library   D. Transit Authority

31. Fustats are likely to be requisitioned MOST frequently by the

    A. Department of Markets   B. Fire Department
    C. Housing Authority   D. Police Department

32. Machine screws are usually purchased in large quantities by the

    A. bushel   B. gross   C. pound   D. score

33. A No. 10 can of fruit juice contains about

    A. eight ounces   B. one pint
    C. one quart   D. three quarts

34. Sulphuric acid is USUALLY purchased in large quantities by the

    A. carboy   B. drum   C. gallon   D. cylinder

35. The one of the following which is NOT a standard size of index card is

    A. 3 x 5   B. 4 x 6   C. 5 x 7   D. 5 x 8

36. The label on a package of mimeograph paper reads: Size 8 1/2 x 11, Basis 20. *Basis 20* refers to the

    A. color code for this type of paper
    B. quality and finish of the paper
    C. way in which the paper is packaged
    D. weight of the paper

37. You tell a man to separate and store cans of paint in a certain way. The man then asks you, *Why do you want me to do it this way?*
You should answer his question by

    A. advising him to figure out the reason himself
    B. explaining to him why you want it done in that particular way
    C. repeating your instructions more slowly
    D. telling him to follow your instructions without asking any questions

38. Assume that an employee shows you that you have made an error in issuing certain instructions. You admit your error.
Such action on your part is desirable PRIMARILY because

    A. the job may be done correctly
    B. your men will be encouraged to make similar corrections in the future
    C. you will gain a reputation for fairness
    D. your men will realize that you will not make errors of this type in the future

39. Assume that you have just been promoted. Your supervisor gives you detailed oral instructions as to how a particular category of stock should be stored. At the conclusion of his instructions, you realize that you do not fully understand how your supervisor wishes to have the stock stored.
Under these circumstances, you should

39._____

    A. ask an experienced worker to clarify your supervisor's instructions
    B. ask your supervisor to clarify anything that you do not understand
    C. ask your supervisor to put his instructions in writing
    D. carry out your supervisor's instructions as best as you can

40. You have reason to believe that one of your men is taking merchandise which does not belong to him from the storehouse. You question the man about this. He tells you that he borrowed the merchandise and intends to return it. Under these Circumstances, you should probably

40._____

    A. disregard the matter until such time as you have evidence which will stand up in court
    B. offer to accompany the man to his home to pick up the property in question
    C. report the matter to your supervisor
    D. tell the man to return the property as soon as he has finished using it

41. A truck which must be unloaded immediately arrives at the storehouse. You issue instructions to your crew as to how this should be done. One of your men strongly objects and says that your instructions are wrong. You listen to his reasons but you still think that you are right. Under these circumstances, you should

41._____

    A. ask for opinions from the other men in the crew as to how the job should be done
    B. contact another worker to get his opinion
    C. refer the matter to your supervisor for his decision
    D. tell the men to unload the truck in accordance with your instructions

42. Whenever you give an assignment to one of your experienced men, he asks you a great many questions about it although he has successfully performed similar assignments in the past. The time you spend in answering his many questions about minor details takes you away from more important work.
Under these circumstances, you should probably FIRST

42._____

    A. answer his questions in such a way that he will be discouraged from asking further questions
    B. ask the man to ask his questions of one of his fellow employees
    C. assure the man of your confidence in his ability to carry out the assignment
    D. tell the man that if the assignment is too difficult you will give it to someone who does not raise so many questions

43. You have reason to believe that one of the men in your crew gossips about you behind your back.
Under these circumstances, it is usually BEST to

43._____

    A. attempt to find out which of your men believes the gossip
    B. find out what the man's weak points are and bring them to the attention of your crew

C. ignore the matter
D. speak to the man about it and tell him to stop

44. Your supervisor gives you an assignment which you believe you cannot do since you do not have a sufficient number of men. You explain this to your supervisor but he tells you to get the job done.
You should

    A. do the best you can and keep your supervisor informed of the progress you are making
    B. report the matter to your main office
    C. insist that your supervisor give you his instructions in writing
    D. wait until your supervisor gives you more men before taking any action to carry out the assignment

44._____

45. Your crew consistently performs more work than the crew headed by another worker. The other worker tells you that the high performance of your crew makes his crew *look bad.*
Under these circumstances, it would be BEST for you to

    A. ignore the matter and have your crew continue working as before
    B. report the matter to your supervisor for disciplinary action
    C. slow your crew down somewhat to show the other man that you are willing to cooperate with him
    D. slow your crew down to the level of the other crew

45._____

46. Two of your men frequently argue with each other so that the work of your crew is disrupted.
You should FIRST

    A. attempt to find out why the men argue with each other
    B. speak to the two men privately regarding their possible transfer to another crew
    C. submit a report to your supervisor setting forth the facts
    D. tell both men that unless they stop arguing you will see that they are given below-standard service ratings

46._____

47. One of your men asks you to put him in for an above-standard service rating. His work has been good but it has not been above-standard.
You should tell the man that

    A. he has done good work but that in your judgment his work has not been above-standard
    B. if you recommend him for an above-standard service rating, you will have to do the same thing for most of the others in your crew
    C. you cannot discuss the matter with him but that you will discuss it with your supervisor
    D. you will speak to the other men in the crew and if no one objects you will recommend him for a higher service rating

47._____

48. You receive a memorandum from your supervisor in which he instructs you to make a large number of changes in the procedures for storing materials.
The BEST way to bring these changes to the attention of your crew is to

    A. post the memorandum on the bulletin board where everyone can read it
    B. meet individually with each member of your staff to discuss the changes
    C. hold a meeting with your crew and explain the changes to them
    D. see to it that the memorandum is circulated to and initialled by each member of the crew

48.____

49. Although you have frequently spoken to one of your men regarding the proper way of lifting heavy objects, he persists in ignoring your instructions. He says that he knows the proper way of lifting, that you do not, and that he does not intend to hurt himself by following your instructions.
Of the following, the BEST course of action for you to take is to

    A. assign the man to tasks which do not involve heavy lifting
    B. ignore the matter as long as the man does not hurt himself
    C. put your instructions on how to lift in writing and give a copy of your instructions to each man in the crew
    D. report the matter to your supervisor

49.____

50. You assign a man to take inventory of a certain item. The man gives you a figure which seems too high. Of the following, the BEST course of action for you to take is to

    A. accept the figure given to you by the man if he is willing to initial it
    B. accompany the man while he takes inventory again
    C. ask the man to take inventory again and tell him why
    D. take inventory yourself

50.____

KEY (CORRECT ANSWERS)

1.	B	11.	B	21.	A	31.	C	41.	D
2.	A	12.	B	22.	C	32.	B	42.	C
3.	B	13.	A	23.	C	33.	D	43.	C
4.	A	14.	D	24.	B	34.	A	44.	A
5.	D	15.	C	25.	C	35.	C	45.	A
6.	A	16.	D	26.	B	36.	D	46.	A
7.	A	17.	C	27.	A	37.	B	47.	A
8.	C	18.	B	28.	A	38.	A	48.	C
9.	C	19.	C	29.	C	39.	B	49.	D
10.	B	20.	A	30.	A	40.	C	50.	C

EXAMINATION SECTION
TEST 1

DIRECTIONS: Each question or incomplete statement is followed by several suggested answers or completions. Select the one that BEST answers the question or completes the statement. *PRINT THE LETTER OF THE CORRECT ANSWER IN THE SPACE AT THE RIGHT.*

1. Of the following, the hazard MOST likely to damage rubber tubes in storage is 1.____
   - A. breakage
   - B. combustion
   - C. corrosion
   - D. deterioration

2. Of the following, the hazard MOST likely to damage vacuum tubes in storage is 2.____
   - A. breakage
   - B. corrosion
   - C. deterioration
   - D. evaporation

3. In checking large numbers of incoming supplies of a single item, the BEST practice to follow is to 3.____
   - A. count the total number of containers received and only count the number of units in some of the containers
   - B. count the total number of containers received only in those shipments where there is some doubt
   - C. open all exterior containers received and count the number of containers inside when there are interior containers
   - D. open all exterior and interior containers received and count the exact number of units

4. Some experts advise that barrels containing liquids should be turned occasionally. The BEST reason for this is to 4.____
   - A. enable a check of the condition of the barrel
   - B. enable a check of the condition of the contents
   - C. keep the contents well mixed
   - D. prevent the wood from drying out

5. For day-to-day protection when working in a room or enclosure containing combustible or explosive gases or gasolines, it would be MOST advisable to wear 5.____
   - A. a general purpose gas mask
   - B. a synthetic rubber suit
   - C. non-sparking shoes
   - D. rubber-framed goggles

6. The one of the following which is NOT recommended as a method of reducing the possibility of spontaneous combustion of burlap bags is to 6.____
   - A. air them out before stacking
   - B. dampen them slightly before stacking
   - C. keep them off concrete floors
   - D. keep them away from brick walls

29

7. When oxygen is leaking from a gas cylinder and the valve cannot close properly, the MOST advisable course of action to take while waiting for the valve to be repaired is to

   A. evacuate the building
   B. have it sent to a using agency before more oxygen is lost
   C. place the cylinder in the room with the poorest ventilation
   D. remove the cylinder from the building

8. Assume that you have to move four cartons to a location about 35 feet away. Each carton weighs 20 pounds and measures 2' x 8' x 4'.
   Of the following, the method of moving the cartons which would ordinarily be BEST is to

   A. have a team of two men make four trips
   B. have two teams of two men each carry two cartons
   C. make one trip using a four-wheel handtruck
   D. make one trip using a two-wheel handtruck

9. Assume that you have to move one carton to a location about 15 feet away. The carton weighs about 30 pounds and measures 8" x 18" x 24".
   Of the following, the method of moving the carton which would ordinarily be BEST is to

   A. have one man carry it
   B. have two men carry it
   C. put it on a two-wheel handtruck
   D. put it on a four-wheel handtruck

10. Assume that you have to move ten 45-pound cartons to a location about 75 feet away. Each carton measures 24" x 24" x 24".
    Of the following, the method of moving the cartons which would ordinarily be BEST is to

    A. load them on a pallet and use a forklift truck
    B. load them on a skid and push the skid
    C. load them on a trailer and pull it with a tractor
    D. use a portable conveyor

Questions 11-16.

DIRECTIONS: Questions 11 through 16 are to be answered SOLELY on the basis of the following table.

3 (#1)

REPORT OF SEMI-ANNUAL INVENTORY

Article	Unit	Physical Inventory Qty.	Price	Amt.	Perpetual Inventory Qty.	Amt.	Adjustment Qty.	Amt.
Batteries, flashlight	ea.	63	.08	5.04	60	14.80	+3	+.24
Bolts, flat head with square nuts, 100 in box	box	23	1.47	33.80	25	36.75		
Fuse, 15 amp, 4 in box	box	80	.07	5.60	80	5.60		
Fuse, 20 amp, 4 in box	box	77	.07	5.39	80	5.60	3	.21
Tape, friction, 50 ft. to a roll	roll	45	.22	9.90	45	9.90		
Washers, 100 in can 1/8" beveled	can	35	.32	11.20	35	11.20		
3/8" beveled	can	41	.33	13.53	45	14.85	4	1.32
Totals				84.47		88.70		

11. In the above report, for which item is there an INCORRECT entry?   11._____

    A. 15 amp. fuses   B. Friction tape
    C. Flashlight batteries   D. 1/8" washers

12. In the above report, adjustments were omitted for _____ article(s).   12._____

    A. one   B. two   C. three   D. four

13. After all appropriate entries have been made in the Adjustment column, the total which must be deducted from the book value of the inventory is   13._____

    A. $1.53   B. $1.77   C. $4.23   D. $4.71

14. The quantities shown in Perpetual Inventory exceed those shown in Physical Inventory by a total of   14._____

    A. 4   B. 6   C. 10   D. 12

15. The cost of ten washers, 1/8" beveled, is MOST NEARLY   15._____

    A. $.003   B. $.032   C. $.320   D. $3.20

16. The cost of 24 fuses is MOST NEARLY   16._____

    A. $.28   B. $.42   C. $.80   D. $1.68

31

17. Assume that you are in charge of a group of four men who are to carry an oak beam measuring 8" x 8" x 18' from one point to another.
Of the following, the BEST method of carrying the beam is to have

   A. the men arrange themselves at equal distances along one side of the beam and carry the beam at their sides
   B. the men arrange themselves at equal distances on opposite sides of the beam and carry the beam at waist height
   C. the men arrange themselves in order of height along the beam so that the beam may be carried on the shoulders of all of the men
   D. two men stand at one end of the beam and two men at the other end in order to lift the beam on to the shoulders of the two strongest men

18. Although the old model of a certain item has been replaced by a new model which is interchangeable with the old model, most requisitions call specifically for the old model. Since your stock of the old model is almost depleted, it would be MOST advisable for you to

   A. establish a carefully regulated system of priorities based on need
   B. inform the source of your supply of the continued demand for the old model
   C. inform the using agencies or individuals of the feasibility of substituting the new model
   D. substitute the new model whenever the old model is called for

19. An assistant stockman is assigned by you to take physical inventory of a particular small part stored in several open boxes. This part is of uniform size and is packaged 100 to a box. He returns in an unusually short time with the count. His explanation for his speed is that he consolidated all the items as much as possible so that all except one box were full. He multiplied 100 by the number of boxes and added the number of additional parts left.
Of the following, the MOST advisable course of action for you to take is to

   A. compliment him on his efficiency
   B. explain the proper way of taking inventory
   C. have him watch a more experienced worker take inventory
   D. suggest that he ask permission before changing procedure

20. In determining the number of months of supply to be ordered at one time, the LEAST important of the following factors is the

   A. average market price
   B. deterioration rate
   C. discount for quantity
   D. money available for purchasing

21. A check during physical inventory has revealed that many of the bottles of alcohol do not contain sixteen ounces as indicated on the labels.
Of the following, the MOST advisable action to take FIRST is to

   A. check future shipments by the vendor immediately upon their arrival
   B. see if the bottles are tightly capped
   C. see if the cartons are wet
   D. question your subordinates about the situation

22. Of the following, the FIRST thing which should be done in order to determine the reason for a discrepancy between the perpetual inventory card and the bin card or other similar record is to

    A. check the original requisitions
    B. compare each transaction listed on both cards
    C. ascertain whether any stock has been transferred to another warehouse
    D. question all personnel involved

23. Items such as tools are sometimes issued on a temporary basis and are to be returned after use so that they may be issued again when needed. In such cases, a record of each withdrawal

    A. need not be kept
    B. should be made on an inventory card
    C. should be made on a locator card
    D. should be made on a separate register

24. Assume that you have 100 boxes of a particular item on hand. Since this is the minimum order point, you have already ordered 300 boxes, which is the usual 6 months' supply. This order has not yet been delivered, and you have just received a requisition for 1,000 boxes.
    Of the following, the MOST advisable action for you to take FIRST is to

    A. order an additional 1,000 boxes
    B. order an additional 1,300 boxes
    C. ascertain the reason for such a requisition
    D. inform the ordering agency that the requisition cannot be filled immediately

Questions 25-27.

   DIRECTIONS: Questions 25 through 27 are based on the following method of obtaining a reorder point: multiply the monthly rate of consumption by the lead time (in months) and add the minimum balance.

25. If the reorder point is 250 units, the lead time is 2 months, and the average monthly rate of consumption is 75 units, then the minimum balance is _____ units.

    A. 75   B. 100   C. 150   D. 250

26. If the lead time is 30 days, the minimum balance is 200 units, and the average monthly rate of consumption is 100 units, then the reorder point is _____ units.

    A. 100   B. 200   C. 300   D. 400

27. If the reorder point is 300 units, the lead time is 2 months, and the minimum balance is 100 units, then the average monthly rate of consumption is _____ units.

    A. 50   B. 100   C. 200   D. 300

28. You are planning to submit an initial order for a new item. You estimate that you will issue 100 per month, and you want to have a two-month supply in reserve. You will reorder this item every six months. Your initial order should be for

    A. 200   B. 600   C. 700   D. 800

29. For a particular item, the reorder point is established at 585.
If the average rate of consumption is 130 and the lead time is 3 months, then the amount which should be on hand when the new delivery is received is

   A. 130   B. 195   C. 260   D. 325

30. You have room in the storehouse for 750 cartons of a certain item. Assume that you issue 125 cartons per month and keep a one-month supply in reserve. Delivery time is thirty days.
Which of the following would it be MOST appropriate to order under these conditions?
_____ every _____ months.

   A. 250; 3   B. 500; 3   C. 375; 4   D. 500; 4

31. Using maximum loads when transporting stock is

   A. *desirable* because it results in fewer trips
   B. *desirable* because it simplifies accounting and clerical work
   C. *undesirable* because it shortens the life of the equipment
   D. *undesirable* because it strains the capacity of the workers

32. Of the following, the BEST single basis for determining the desirability of purchasing new stock-handling equipment is the

   A. ability of the workers to handle the equipment
   B. condition of the present equipment
   C. estimated savings in costs
   D. size of the warehouse or stock facility

33. Frequent rest periods are MOST desirable when

   A. the men have been doing a good job
   B. the morale of the men is low
   C. there is a great deal of heavy work
   D. there is not too much work

34. In terms of plant economy, a storehouse is operating at GREATEST efficiency when it stores _____ stock that it is designed to hold.

   A. 10% less   B. 10% more
   C. 50% more   D. the exact amount of

35. Of the following, the one which a foreman or supervisor can MOST readily increase or improve is an employee's ability to

   A. get along with his fellow workers
   B. perform technical aspects of his job
   C. supervise others
   D. use good judgment in unusual situations

36. On one day, a certain piece of stock-handling equipment is not used at all. On the next day, several men are waiting to use it.
This situation can BEST be corrected by

   A. having the men do the work manually
   B. keeping additional equipment available

C. posting a schedule for the use of the equipment
D. rearranging the work of the men

37. Despite all your efforts to streamline the work and make it more efficient, there still seems to be more work than you and your men can handle in a normal work week.
The MOST advisable course of action for you to take FIRST is to

   A. discuss the matter with your supervisor
   B. request more mechanical equipment
   C. request permission for overtime work
   D. tell your men that everyone will have to work a little harder

37.____

38. Assume that a subordinate tells you that he has made a mistake in filling out certain records.
The MOST advisable action for you to take FIRST is to

   A. explain how the job should have been done
   B. get another subordinate to do the job correctly
   C. tell him how to correct his mistake
   D. tell him to forget it but to do it correctly next time

38.____

39. Your supervisor gives you instructions which you feel are contrary to good storage procedure.
The MOST advisable action for you to take FIRST is to

   A. attempt to get additional support for your point of view
   B. follow his instructions without question
   C. suggest your method of doing the work
   D. say nothing but do the job the way you feel it should be done

39.____

40. You have reason to believe that one of your men is taking home merchandise from the storehouse. You question the man about this. He shows you that it was obsolete material of no value which was not salvageable and was about to be discarded.
Under these circumstances, the MOST appropriate action for you to take is to

   A. have him return the merchandise
   B. report the matter to your supervisor
   C. say nothing further
   D. tell the man that he should have asked your permission

40.____

41. Three new men have just been assigned to work under your supervision. Every time you give them an assignment, one of these men asks you several questions.
Of the following, the MOST advisable action for you to take is to

   A. assure him of your confidence in his ability to carry out the assignment correctly without asking so many questions
   B. have all three men listen to your answers to these questions
   C. point out that the other two men do the job without asking so many questions
   D. tell him to see if he can get the answers from other workers before coming to you

41.____

42. One of the men in your crew has continually been making derogatory statements about the personal life of one of the other men.
Of the following, it would probably be MOST advisable for you to

   A. attempt to obtain a transfer for the man who is the subject of the derogatory statements
   B. ignore the matter unless it has any effect on the work
   C. point out to your crew some of the weak spots in the character of the man who is making derogatory statements
   D. tell the man to stop making derogatory statements

43. Two of your subordinates suggest that you recommend a third man for an above-standard service rating because of his superior work.
You should

   A. ask the two subordinates whether the third man knows that they intended to discuss this matter with you
   B. explain to the two subordinates that an above-standard service rating for one man would have a detrimental effect on many of the other men
   C. recommend the man for an above-standard service rating if there is sufficient justification for it
   D. tell the two subordinates that the matter of service ratings is not their concern

44. At a meeting with your subordinates, which you have called in order to determine the best ways of dealing with some departmental policies, some of the men interrupt with comments and suggestions.
Of the following, the MOST advisable course of action for you to take in MOST cases is to

   A. encourage full but orderly participation by all the men
   B. end the meeting and issue a bulletin instead
   C. tell them to hold their comments and questions until after you have finished
   D. tell those who interrupt that they are being unfair to the others

45. When one of your subordinates takes unusually long lunch hours, you tell him that this practice must stop.
Of the following, the BEST reason for speaking to him about this is that

   A. he will take even longer lunch hours unless you speak to him
   B. morale of your other subordinates may be impaired unless the situation is corrected
   C. work cannot be done in time unless the practice is discontinued
   D. your other subordinates will take the same amount of time for lunch as he does

46. You have just been assigned a new employee who has had a college education but has had no experience in stock work. Of the following, the BEST course of action for you to take is to

   A. attempt to have him transferred as soon as possible
   B. explain to him that he probably would not like the work
   C. make special efforts to ease his relationships with the other workers
   D. treat him the same as you would treat any other new worker

47. The morale of your subordinates seems unusually high. They tell you that it is because they have heard that one of them is to get a provisional promotion. You know definitely that this is not true.
The MOST advisable action for you to take is to

   A. act as if you are happy to hear the good news
   B. let the situation take its normal course
   C. report the matter to your supervisor
   D. tell them that, so far as you know, the rumor is not justified

48. In most cases, the FIRST step to take in the event of serious injury in the storeroom is to

   A. search the employee for instructions pertaining to medical care
   B. send for medical help
   C. take the employee to a hospital
   D. treat the injury

49. An employee has accidentally cut his arm and is bleeding profusely.
The one of the following which should NOT be done is to

   A. apply pressure above the injury
   B. give the employee a mild stimulant
   C. keep the employee at complete rest
   D. raise the bleeding part

50. When gasoline and all other highly inflammable substances are stored outdoors, the *No Smoking* rule should be

   A. observed for indoor and outdoor storage areas
   B. observed for indoor storage areas only
   C. observed for outdoor storage areas only
   D. eliminated for indoor and outdoor storage areas

KEY (CORRECT ANSWERS)

1. D	11. C	21. B	31. A	41. B
2. A	12. A	22. B	32. C	42. D
3. A	13. C	23. D	33. C	43. C
4. D	14. B	24. C	34. D	44. A
5. C	15. B	25. B	35. B	45. B
6. B	16. B	26. C	36. D	46. D
7. D	17. A	27. B	37. A	47. D
8. C	18. C	28. D	38. C	48. B
9. A	19. A	29. B	39. C	49. B
10. A	20. A	30. D	40. D	50. A

EXAMINATION SECTION
TEST 1

DIRECTIONS: Each question or incomplete statement is followed by several suggested answers or completions. Select the one that BEST answers the question or completes the statement. *PRINT THE LETTER OF THE CORRECT ANSWER IN THE SPACE AT THE RIGHT.*

1. Of the following, the MOST efficient way to handle and store heavy objects loaded on pallets in a warehouse is with the aid of a   1.____

   A. conveyor belt   B. hand truck
   C. dolly   D. forklift

2. You receive 20 large glass containers of highly dangerous acid.   2.____
   Of the following, it would be SAFEST to store these glass containers in _____ area.

   A. a special designated   B. a busy workshop
   C. the main storage   D. the shipping and receiving

Questions 3-7.

DIRECTIONS: Questions 3 through 7 each contains a description of a stock item which is incomplete. You are to answer each question by selecting the term which BEST completes the description of the item.

> EXAMPLE: Brush, tooth, adult size
> A. nylon bristle
> B. glass handle
> C. 18 inches
> D. fluoride
>
> The CORRECT answer is A, which completes the description of a toothbrush.

3. Polish, furniture, one quart can   3.____

   A. gasoline   B. acid
   C. lemon oil   D. glue substance

4. Card, index, ruled, white   4.____

   A. bond   B. 3" x 5"   C. round   D. plastic

5. Sugar, 1/6 ounce, individual package   5.____

   A. soft   B. mixed   C. sprinkled   D. granulated

6. Pad, gauze, 2 in. x 2 in.   6.____

   A. sterile   B. paper   C. rubber   D. cold

7. Shovel, snow, square point   7.____

   A. sweeper   B. duster   C. long handle   D. saw tooth

39

8. There are times when birds find their way into a warehouse and make nests. This may cause problems to the store-keeping operations.
Of the following, the MOST practical way to deal with this matter is to _____ the warehouse.

   A. place bird feed outside
   B. plant trees around
   C. provide bird perches in
   D. destroy bird nests in

9. Entries of incoming and outgoing stock items are made on individual stock cards for all the following reasons EXCEPT

   A. detecting possible stealing of the stock items
   B. keeping an accurate record of the stock items
   C. officially recording the entries of incoming and outgoing stock items
   D. showing your supervisor what a good job you can do

10. A particular stock item presently shows an inventory balance smaller than the inventory balance of the previous month.
Of the following, this information shows you that the quantity of this particular item

    A. issued was more than the amount received
    B. issued was less than the amount received
    C. received was equal to the amount issued
    D. received was more than the amount issued

Questions 11-12.

DIRECTIONS: Questions 11 and 12 are to be answered on the basis of the information given in the following passage relating to an Executive Order by the Mayor.

The Commissioner of Investigation shall have general responsibility for the investigation and elimination of corrupt or other criminal activity, conflicts of interest, unethical conduct, misconduct, and incompetence by city agencies, by city officers and employees, and by persons regulated by, doing business with, or receiving funds directly or indirectly from the city, with respect to their dealings with the city. All agency heads shall be responsible for establishing, subject to review for completeness and inter-agency consistency by the Commissioner of Investigation, written standards of conduct for the officials and employees of their respective agencies, and fair and efficient disciplinary systems to maintain those standards of conduct. All agencies shall have an Inspector General who shall report directly to the respective agency head and to the Commissioner of Investigation and be responsible for maintaining standards of conduct as may be established in such agency under this Order. Inspectors General shall be responsible for the investigation and elimination of corrupt or other criminal activity, conflicts of interest, unethical conduct, misconduct and incompetence within their respective agencies. Except to the extent otherwise provided by law, the employment or continued employment of all existing and prospective Inspectors General and members of their staffs shall be subject to complete background investigations and approval by the Department of Investigation.

11. According to the above passage, establishing written standards of conduct for each agency is the responsibility of the

   A. agency head
   B. Commissioner of Investigation
   C. Department of Investigation
   D. Inspector General

11._____

12. According to the above passage, maintaining standards of conduct within each agency is the responsibility of the

   A. agency head
   B. Commissioner of Investigation
   C. Department of Investigation
   D. Inspector General

12._____

Questions 13-16.

DIRECTIONS: Questions 13 through 16 are to be answered on the basis of the following information.

Assume that Warehouse X uses the following procedures for receiving stock. When a delivery is received, the stock handler who receives the delivery should immediately unpack and check the delivery. This check is to ensure that the quantity and kinds of stock items delivered match those on the purchase order which had been sent to the vendor. After the delivery is checked, a receiving report is prepared by the same stock handler. This receiving report should include the name of the shipper, the purchase order number, the description of the item, and the actual count or weight of the item. The receiving report, along with the packing slip, should then be checked by the stores clerk against the purchase order to make sure that the quantity received is correct. This is necessary before credit can be obtained from the vendor for any items that are missing or damaged. After the checking is completed, the stock items can be moved to the stockroom.

13. According to the procedures described above, the stock person who receives the delivery should

   A. placed the unopened delivery in a secure area for checking at a later date
   B. notify the stores clerk that the delivery has arrived and is ready for checking
   C. unpack the delivery and check the quantity and types of stock items against the purchase order
   D. closely examine the outside of the delivery containers for dents and damages

13._____

14. According to the procedures described above, credit can be obtained from the vendor

   A. *before* the stock handler checks the delivery of stock items
   B. *after* the stock handler checks the delivery of stock items
   C. *before* the stores clerk checks the receiving report against the purchase order
   D. *after* the stores clerk checks the receiving report against the purchase order

14._____

15. According to the procedures described above, all of the following information should be included when filling out a receiving report EXCEPT the

   A. purchase order number
   B. name of the shipper
   C. count or weight of the item
   D. unit cost per item

16. According to the procedures described above, after the stores clerk has checked the receiving report against the purchase order, the NEXT step is to

   A. move the stock items to the stockroom
   B. return the stock items received to the vendor
   C. give the stock items to the stock handler for final checking
   D. file the packing slip for inventory purposes

17. All of the following would be good ways for you to show an employee how to pack a box EXCEPT

   A. making sure that the employee can clearly see what you are doing
   B. going through the process slowly and carefully with the employee
   C. talking and working as quickly as you can, so that you don't bore the employee
   D. explaining the purpose of each step to the employee

18. You are starting to prepare a requisition for certain supplies, which must be done as soon as possible. A co-worker comes to you and asks you for your help in finding several stock items. You are told that finding these items will take some time. You decide to finish preparing the requisition first before you help your co-worker.
    Of the following, your action can BEST be described as

   A. *acceptable* because you must prepare the requisition as quickly as possible
   B. *unacceptable* because you should help your co-worker
   C. *acceptable* because your co-worker should be able to do the job alone
   D. *unacceptable* because you can finish preparing the requisition some other time

19. A newly-hired employee has just been assigned to work under your supervision. You want to be sure that the employee will do the job well and perform it properly. Of the following, the FIRST action you should take is to

   A. tell the employee exactly what has to be done and what is expected
   B. allow the employee to begin work on a difficult task immediately
   C. assign the employee to work with others who have little experience
   D. give the employee enough work to keep busy

20. You observe two of your subordinates, Mr. White and Mr. Wilson, lifting heavy items together. You see that Mr. White is not lifting the items properly while Mr. Wilson is. As the supervisor, the MOST appropriate action for you to take in this situation is to

   A. allow Mr. White time to learn by himself the correct way to lift heavy items
   B. have Mr. Wilson lift the heavy items by himself
   C. show Mr. White how to lift the heavy items properly
   D. advise Mr. Wilson to be very careful when working with Mr. White

21. One of your subordinates asks you to meet with him privately to discuss a personal problem which he feels is affecting his work performance. You know that you have a very busy work schedule every day.
As the supervisor, the BEST way for you to handle this situation is to

    A. tell the subordinate that you are too busy to meet with him today but to try again in a few days
    B. tell the subordinate that it is not proper to discuss personal problems
    C. schedule a meeting with the subordinate for that same day
    D. tell the subordinate that you will hold a group meeting soon to discuss any problems

22. One of your responsibilities as a supervisor is to make sure that the unit area is cleaned up each day. You know that no one in your unit likes to do the cleaning. In order to minimize any dissatisfaction on the part of your subordinates, it would be BEST for you to assign this work

    A. to the strongest worker in your unit
    B. on a rotating basis
    C. to the slowest worker in your unit
    D. on a disciplinary basis

23. Two of your subordinates approach you and ask you to help them with a disagreement they are having about their job duties.
The BEST approach for you to take in dealing with this situation is to

    A. tell the subordinates they should be able to settle the disagreement themselves
    B. check with other subordinates to find out if they can be of any help
    C. tell the subordinates to return to work and not to discuss the matter any further
    D. listen to what each subordinate has to say and then try to help them to reach an agreement

24. Assume that food items, as they are received, are clearly dated on the outside of each package by the receiver.
If you assign one of your subordinates to pick the oldest stock of food items first when filling an order, then you should expect the subordinate to find the oldest stock by

    A. checking the date on the outside of each package
    B. opening each package and checking the items inside
    C. getting the information from the receiver
    D. asking you for the information

25. One of your subordinates has been arriving at work about one-half hour late every day for the past two weeks. However, the subordinate is able to complete the work on time and continues to do a good job.
As the supervisor, the BEST way for you to deal with this matter is to

    A. talk to the subordinate in private about the lateness
    B. praise the subordinate for the good work being done
    C. say nothing because the subordinate is still doing the job well
    D. ask your superior what you should do

26. Assume that you have outlined four steps you are going to take in solving a storekeeping problem. These steps are as follows:
   I. Analyze the facts.
   II. Define the problem.
   III. List possible solutions.
   IV. Get the facts.

   Which one of the following shows the order of taking these steps that would be MOST effective in solving a problem?

   A. IV, II, I, III
   B. II, IV, I, III
   C. III, I, II, IV
   D. I, III, II, IV

Questions 27-31.

DIRECTIONS: Questions 27 through 31 are to be answered on the basis of the information given in Tables 1 and 2 of the DAILY PRODUCTIVITY REPORT shown below.

DAILY PRODUCTIVITY REPORT

Table 1

Standards Number of pieces packed per day	Unsatisfactory	Conditional	Satisfactory	Superior	Outstanding
	245 and below	246 to 289	290 to 347	348 to 405	406 and above

Table 2

Initials of the Packer	A.S	S.B.	B.D	L.M.	J.C	R.N.	B.G	C.A	D.F	E.R
Number of Pieces Packed Per Day	252	335	276	342	409	290	235	309	246	425

27. The number of packers whose productivity is *Outstanding* is

   A. 4   B. 3   C. 2   D. 1

28. The number of packers who come under the *Conditional* productivity standard is

   A. 1   B. 2   C. 3   D. 4

29. The percentage of packers whose productivity can be rated *Satisfactory* or higher is

   A. 30%   B. 40%   C. 50%   D. 60%

30. If every packer's daily productivity increased by 20 pieces, the number of packers whose productivity ratings would change to the NEXT standard is

   A. 4   B. 5   C. 6   D. 7

31. Which one of the following is an accurate statement that can be made based on the information shown in Tables 1 and 2?

   A. There are more packers whose productivity is above the maximum *Satisfactory* level than below the minimum *Satisfactory* level.
   B. There are more packers whose productivity is in the *Satisfactory* standard than in any one of the other four standards.
   C. The number of packers whose productivity is *Unsatisfactory* is equal to the number of packers whose productivity is *Outstanding*.
   D. There is at least one packer whose productivity is in each of the five standards.

Questions 32-35.

DIRECTIONS: Questions 32 through 35 are to be answered on the basis of the information given in the inventory tables shown below. Table 1 shows the amount of each item in stock according to the information contained on the perpetual inventory card for that item. Table 2 shows the amount of the same item in stock according to an inventory just completed by the staff.

Table 1

Perpetual Inventory Card	
Item No.	Amount of Stock
A107	2,564
A257	10,365
A342	7,018
A475	52,475
B026	16,207
B422	4,520
B717	21,431
B802	308
C328	594
C329	164
C438	723
C527	844

Table 2

Inventory Just Completed By Staff	
Item No.	Amount of Stock
A107	2,545
A257	10,356
A342	7,018
A475	52,475
B026	16,207
B422	4,505
B717	21,413
B802	308
C328	594
C329	143
C438	723
C527	854

32. In which one of the following items is there a difference between the amount of stock shown on the perpetual inventory card and in the inventory just completed?
    Item No.

    A. A257   B. B026   C. C328   D. C438

33. In which one of the following items is the difference GREATEST between the amount of stock shown on the perpetual inventory card and in the inventory just completed?
    Item No.

    A. A107   B. B422   C. B717   D. C329

34. The amount of stock shown for Item No. C527 on the inventory taken by the staff is greater than the amount shown on the perpetual inventory card.
Of the following, the LEAST likely reason for this difference is that the

   A. perpetual inventory card was not brought up to date
   B. staff did not take an accurate inventory
   C. information entered on the perpetual inventory card was inaccurate
   D. staff made an inventory on the wrong item

35. Which one of the following is an ACCURATE statement that can be made based on the information shown in Tables 1 and 2?

   A. More than half of the items listed show a difference between the amount of stock shown on the perpetual inventory card and in the inventory just completed.
   B. One-third of the items listed show the amount of stock on the perpetual inventory card and in the inventory just completed to be 10,000 or more.
   C. Less than half of the items listed show a difference between the amount of stock shown on the perpetual inventory card and in the inventory just completed.
   D. One-third of the items listed show the amount of stock on the perpetual inventory card and in the inventory just completed to be 10,000 or less.

36. You are preparing to hold a training session for your unit on the safe use of storekeeping equipment.
Of the following, the MOST important reason for you to give this training is to

   A. answer any questions your workers may have about the use of the equipment
   B. speed up the work done by the unit
   C. reduce the amount of time lost for equipment repair
   D. prevent accidents from happening when the equipment is being used

37. Of the following, the use of an A frame storage rack is MOST appropriate for storing

   A. pipes or tubular items
   B. crated goods
   C. office supplies and equipment
   D. empty pallets

38. Your warehouse is infested by rats. You have asked one of your subordinates to place rat traps throughout the warehouse in order to take care of the problem.
Of the following, the BEST way to use traps effectively is to

   A. keep the same bait in the traps at all times
   B. change the location of the traps frequently
   C. disinfect the unused traps daily
   D. place the traps in the busiest work areas

39. Of the following, the BEST way to determine how much of a certain item should be ordered each month is to

   A. call the vendor of a similar item to find out how often that item is delivered to your agency
   B. call another agency to find out how often deliveries of that item are made to that agency

C. keep an ongoing record of how much of the item is used during each month
D. increase the usual order so that your agency will never run out of that item

40. According to the information on a computer run, your stock of distilled water is short by 20 gallons. Of the following, the FIRST appropriate action you should take is to

    A. check your own records of all the deliveries and issuances
    B. let the computer unit know of their mistake
    C. balance the shortage by showing an issuance of 20 gallons in the next report
    D. buy 20 gallons of distilled water to make up the shortage

40.____

KEY (CORRECT ANSWERS)

1.	D	11.	A	21.	C	31.	B
2.	A	12.	D	22.	B	32.	A
3.	C	13.	C	23.	D	33.	D
4.	B	14.	D	24.	A	34.	D
5.	D	15.	D	25.	A	35.	B
6.	A	16.	A	26.	B	36.	D
7.	C	17.	C	27.	C	37.	A
8.	D	18.	A	28.	C	38.	B
9.	D	19.	A	29.	D	39.	C
10.	A	20.	C	30.	A	40.	A

TEST 2

DIRECTIONS: Each question or incomplete statement is followed by several suggested answers or completions. Select the one that BEST answers the question or completes the statement. *PRINT THE LETTER OF THE CORRECT ANSWER IN THE SPACE AT THE RIGHT.*

Questions 1-3.

DIRECTIONS: Questions 1 through 3 are to be answered on the basis of the information given in the passage below.

A filing system for requisition forms used in a warehouse will be of maximum benefit only if it provides ready access to information needed and is not too complex. How effective the system will be depends largely on how well the filing system is organized. A well-organized system usually results in a smooth-running operation.

When setting up a system for filing requisition forms, one effective method would be to first make an alphabetical listing of all the authorized requisitioning agencies. Then file folders should be prepared for each of these agencies and arranged alphabetically in file cabinets. Following this, each agency should be assigned a series of numbers corresponding to those on the blank requisition forms with which they will be supplied. When an agency then submits a requisition and it is filled, the form should be filed in numerical order in the designated agency folder. By using this system, any individual requisition form which is missing from its folder can be easily detected. Regardless of the filing system used, simplicity is essential if the filing system is to be successful.

1. According to the above passage, a filing system is MOST likely to be successful if it is   1.____

   A. alphabetical   B. uncomplicated
   C. numerical   D. reliable

2. According to the above passage, the reason numbers are assigned to each agency is to   2.____

   A. simplify stock issuing procedures
   B. keep a count of all incoming requisition forms
   C. be able to know when a form is missing from its folder
   D. eliminate the need for an alphabetical filing system

3. According to the above passage, which one of the following is an ACCURATE statement regarding the establishment of a well-organized filing system?   3.____

   A. Requisitioned stock items will be issued at a faster rate.
   B. Stock items will be stored in storage areas alphabetically arranged.
   C. Information concerning ordered stock items will be easily obtainable.
   D. Maximum productivity can be expected from each employee.

Questions 4-6.

DIRECTIONS: Questions 4 through 6 are to be answered on the basis of the information given in the chart below.

ITEM NUMBER TOTALS AS OF JANUARY 31

Item Number	Monthly Usage	Current Inventory	Time Required Between Ordering & Delivery of Item
1	460	1,000	1 month
2	475	1,500	2 months
3	225	1,500	4 months
4	500	2,500	5 months
5	1,150	1,950	2 months
6	775	4,700	5 months
7	850	1,700	2 months
8	900	3,600	3 months
9	175	525	2 months
10	1,325	5,300	3 months
11	225	900	4 months
12	425	1,500	1 month

4. Which one of the following, if not ordered by February 1, would cause the monthly usage to exceed the current inventory before new merchandise could be received?
Item Number

   A. 1   B. 4   C. 6   D. 10

5. Which one of the following must be ordered immediately because the current inventory cannot cover the monthly usage?
Item Number

   A. 2   B. 3   C. 5   D. 12

6. The date by which Item Numbers 8, 9, and 10 must be ordered so that the monthly usage does NOT exceed the current inventory is _____ .

   A. February 1   B. March 1
   C. April 1   D. May 1

7. When reviewing the monthly management report given to you by the supervisors of the units for which you are responsible, you find that one of the units has a large backlog of unfilled requisitions.
Of the following, the FIRST appropriate action you should take in handling this matter is to

   A. order more stock of all the items stored in your warehouse
   B. check with the supervisors of the other units and see how they would handle the matter
   C. immediately hire more workers to take care of the backlog
   D. consult with the supervisor of the unit which has the backlog to try to find the reason for it

8. You are assigning one of your subordinates, Mr. Jones, to do a task that he has never done before. It is important that he learn how to perform this task as soon as possible, but you do not have the time to train him. You decide to have a highly qualified subordinate, Mr. Smith, show him what must be done.
Of the following, your action concerning this situation can BEST be described as

   A. *acceptable* because it is appropriate for a supervisor to delegate work to a capable subordinate
   B. *unacceptable* because the training must be done by you, the supervisor
   C. *acceptable* because Mr. Smith can do a better job of training Mr. Jones than you can
   D. *unacceptable* because Mr. Smith will not be able to finish his regular duties

9. Jim Johnson has been on your staff for over four years. He has always been a conscientious and productive worker. About a month ago, his wife died; and since that time, his work performance has been very poor.
As his supervisor, which one of the following is the BEST way for you to deal with this situation?

   A. Allow Jim as much time as he needs to overcome his grief and hope that his work performance improves.
   B. Meet with Jim to discuss ways to improve his performance.
   C. Tell Jim directly that you are more concerned with his work performance than with his personal problem.
   D. Prepare disciplinary action on Jim as soon as possible.

10. You are responsible for the overall operation of a storehouse which is divided into two sections. Each section has its own supervisor. You have decided to make several complex changes in the storekeeping procedures which will affect both sections.
Of the following, the BEST way to make sure that these changes are understood by the two supervisors is for you to

    A. meet with both supervisors to discuss the changes
    B. issue a memorandum to each supervisor explaining the changes
    C. post the changes where the supervisors are sure to see them
    D. instruct one supervisor to explain the changes to the other supervisor

11. You have called a meeting of all your subordinates to tell them what has to be done on a new project in which they will all be involved. Several times during the meeting, you ask if there are any questions about what you have told them.
Of the following, to ask the subordinates whether there are any questions during the meeting can BEST be described as

    A. *inadvisable* because it interferes with their learning about the new project
    B. *advisable* because you will find out what they don't understand and have a chance to clear up any problems they may have
    C. *inadvisable* because it makes the meeting too long and causes the subordinates to lose interest in the new project
    D. *advisable* because it gives you a chance to learn which of your subordinates are paying attention to what you say

12. As a supervisor, you are responsible for seeing to it that absenteeism does not become a problem among your subordinates.
   Which one of the following is NOT an acceptable way of controlling the problem of excessive absences?

   A. Distribute a written statement to your staff on the policies regarding absenteeism in your organization.
   B. Arrange for workers who have the fewest absences to talk to those workers who have the most absences.
   C. Let your subordinates know that a record is being kept of all absences.
   D. Arrange for counseling of those employees who are frequently absent.

13. One of your supervisors has been an excellent worker for the past two years. There are no promotion opportunities for this worker in the forseeable future. Due to the city's present budget crisis, a salary increase is not possible.
   Under the circumstances, which one of the following actions on your part would be MOST likely to continue to motivate this worker?

   A. Tell the worker that times are bad all over and jobs are hard to find.
   B. Give the worker less work and easier assignments.
   C. Tell the worker to try to look for a better paying job elsewhere.
   D. Seek the worker's advice often and show that the suggestions provided are appreciated.

14. As a supervisor in a warehouse, it is important that you use your available work force to its fullest potential. Which one of the following actions on your part is MOST likely to increase the effectiveness of your work force?

   A. Assigning more workers to a job than the number actually needed.
   B. Eliminating all job training to allow more time for work output.
   C. Using your best workers on jobs that average workers can do.
   D. Making sure that all materials and equipment used are maintained in good working order.

15. You learn that your storage area will soon be undergoing changes which will affect the work of your subordinates. You decide not to tell your subordinates about what is to happen.
   Of the following, your action can BEST be described as

   A. *wise* because your subordinates will learn of the changes for themselves
   B. *unwise* because your subordinates should be advised about what is to happen
   C. *wise* because it is better for your subordinates to continue working without being disturbed by such news
   D. *unwise* because the work of your subordinates will gradually slow down

16. In making plans for the operation of your unit, you are MOST likely to see these plans carried out successfully if you

   A. allow your staff to participate in developing these plans
   B. do not spend any time on the minor details of these plans
   C. base these plans on the past experiences of others
   D. allow these plans to interact with outside activities in other units

17. A colorless, odorless, and toxic gas that is contained in the exhausts of almost all internal combustion engines is

   A. nitrogen
   B. oxygen
   C. carbon monoxide
   D. sulphur dioxide

18. According to the New York City Fire Code, the recommended clearance from the top of stored warehouse goods to the sprinkler heads must be a minimum of _____ inches.

   A. 2   B. 6   C. 12   D. 18

19. According to the City Fire Code, the recommended width of aisle space in a storage area must be a minimum of _____ foot(feet).

   A. 1   B. 2   C. 3   D. 4

20. As a supervisor in charge of the total operation of a food supply warehouse, you find vandalism to be a potentially serious problem. On occasion, trespassers have gained entrance into the facility by climbing over an unprotected 8-foot fence surrounding the warehouse whose dimensions measure 100 feet by 100 feet.
Assuming that all of the following would be equally effective ways in preventing these breaches in security in the situation described above, which one would be LEAST costly?

   A. Using two trained guard dogs to roam freely throughout the facility at night.
   B. Hiring a security guard to patrol the facility after working hours.
   C. Installing tape razor wire on top of the fence surrounding the facility.
   D. Installing an electronic burglar alarm system requiring the installation of a new fence.

21. Assume that you are considering training one of your subordinates, Mr. Parks, to help you with your record keeping duties. You have decided on using the following four steps in your instruction:
   I. Show Mr. Parks what has to be done.
   II. Find out what Mr. Parks knows about the job.
   III. Check to see how Mr. Parks is doing the job.
   IV. Have Mr. Parks do the job himself.
Which one of the following shows the order of taking these steps that would be MOST effective in training Mr. Parks?

   A. II, I, IV, III
   B. III, II, I, IV
   C. I, IV, III, II
   D. IV, I, II, III

22. The one of the following which provides for efficient storage of loose hardware items such as nails, screws, nuts, bolts, and washers is a(n)

   A. wire mesh basket
   B. metal stack bin
   C. open shelf unit
   D. 55-gallon drum

23. A pallet load template is used to

   A. construct new pallets
   B. determine the floor load capacity in a warehouse
   C. determine the size of the pallet needed for different-sized cartons
   D. increase the allowable floor load in a warehouse

24. The fire extinguisher which is a pump-type tank water unit is used for fires involving all of the following EXCEPT   24.____

    A. wood   B. paper   C. plastic   D. grease

25. When storing 55-gallon drums outdoors, it is BEST to place the drums on their sides in order to   25.____

    A. make them easier to store
    B. prevent rain water from collecting on their tops
    C. allow them to be stacked higher
    D. keep the aisle space smaller

26. In the storage of a flammable liquid, the vapor density of the liquid is the MOST important factor in determining the   26.____

    A. type of fire extinguisher to use
    B. type of container used for storage
    C. location of the ventilating outlets
    D. usable life of a product

27. Of the following, the BEST place to store partially loaded pallets is   27.____

    A. under fully loaded pallets
    B. over other partially loaded pallets
    C. on the top of stacked pallets
    D. in the aisle space between two rows of stacked pallets

28. Of the following, the BEST reason why there should be a clearance on all sides of a stack of loaded pallets is to prevent the   28.____

    A. tipping of the stack
    B. crushing of the lower pallets
    C. collection of moisture in between the stacks
    D. dislocation of the surrounding stacks

29. Where forklift equipment is available, dunnage strips are MOST useful for which one of the following?   29.____

    A. Storing a variety of stock items on loaded pallets
    B. Stacking large containers, boxes, and crates
    C. Storing pipes or other round items
    D. Stacking items to be stored on shelves for a long time

30. Of the following, the MAIN advantage in the use of an *A* frame storage rack is that it provides   30.____

    A. storage space for extremely large supplies of any item
    B. storage space for any item that is to be shipped out immediately
    C. a quick access to items that have to be inspected
    D. maximum accessibility to smaller lots of bulk supplies

31. Which one of the following can be used to provide an efficient means of storing and stacking items that do not readily lend themselves to direct stacking?
A

   A. pallet spear
   B. collapsible pallet box
   C. skid
   D. two-way entry pallet

32. Of the following, the MAJOR benefit of good housekeeping in a warehouse is that it

   A. allows workers more time to perform their regular duties
   B. reduces the need for fire prevention and safety precautions
   C. conserves space, equipment, time, and effort
   D. reduces the need for identifying stock items and storage areas

33. Which one of the following is a good warehouse practice when receiving goods which will require inspection and tests?

   A. Put the goods aside and have them properly labelled.
   B. Leave the goods on the loading dock.
   C. Place the goods into stock without delay.
   D. Issue the goods to the user.

34. The one of the following which is a MAJOR advantage of a power-driven belt conveyor over a gravity-roller conveyor is that a power-driven belt conveyor can

   A. be operated manually with equal effectiveness
   B. move loads from a lower level to a higher level
   C. be operated at any angle
   D. be easily extended by adding sections

35. Of the following, the PRIMARY purpose for using pallets in handling stock is to provide

   A. a large floor load capacity in a warehouse
   B. easy storage of irregular items in a warehouse
   C. efficient handling and storing of material in a warehouse
   D. a safe working environment in a warehouse

36. Of the following, the FIRST consideration in determining whether a particular piece of materials handling equipment should be purchased for use in a large warehouse is the

   A. qualifications of the personnel using the equipment
   B. reliability of the manufacturer
   C. availability of the replacement parts
   D. allowable floor load capacity

37. When a shipment of goods is made to a warehouse, the person receiving the shipment should check the shipment against the freight bill or bill of lading.
The one of the following that thr receiver should note and sign for on the freight bill or bill of lading is the

   A. size of the packages in the shipment
   B. overage, shortage, or damage to the goods
   C. outside identification on the packages
   D. remaining number of shipments to be made

38. In planning how to handle the receipt of goods from a vendor efficiently, which one of the following would be the MOST useful information to have?
The

    A. unit price of the goods to be delivered
    B. cost for shipping the goods
    C. estimated time of arrival and the size of the delivery
    D. type of material used in packing the goods

38.____

39. A using agency has just notified you that they will no longer be using a certain item due to changes in the agency's functions. There is a large supply of this item on hand in your warehouse, and two routine shipments are due next month from the vendor.
Of the following, the MOST advisable action for you to take FIRST in this situation is to

    A. determine if other city warehouses can use these supplies
    B. store the supplies in an inactive section of the warehouse
    C. prepare relinquishment forms to remove existing supplies for resale by the city
    D. notify the proper authority to cancel any orders not yet received

39.____

40. A decision has been made to computerize your warehouse inventory control operation. Upon receiving your first computer readout, you notice that it indicates a shortage of a stock item that is usually in good supply.
Of the following, the FIRST step you should take to deal with this matter is to

    A. make a report of a possible theft
    B. report to the computer center that they are in error
    C. verify the information used for the computer readout
    D. request that the computer be repaired

40.____

KEY (CORRECT ANSWERS)

1.	B	11.	B	21.	A	31.	A
2.	C	12.	B	22.	B	32.	C
3.	C	13.	D	23.	C	33.	A
4.	B	14.	D	24.	D	34.	B
5.	C	15.	B	25.	B	35.	C
6.	B	16.	A	26.	C	36.	D
7.	D	17.	C	27.	C	37.	B
8.	A	18.	D	28.	D	38.	C
9.	B	19.	C	29.	B	39.	D
10.	A	20.	C	30.	D	40.	C

CODING

COMMENTARY

An ingenious question-type called coding, involving elements of alphabetizing, filing, name and number comparison, and evaluative judgment and application, has currently won wide acceptance in testing circles for measuring clerical aptitude and general ability, particularly on the senior (middle) grades (levels).

While the directions for this question usually vary in detail, the candidate is generally asked to consider groups of names, codes, and numbers, and, then, according to a given plan, to arrange codes in alphabetic order; to arrange these in numerical sequence; to rearrange columns of names and numbers in correct order; to espy errors in coding; to choose the correct coding arrangement in consonance with the given directions and examples, etc.

This question-type appears to have few paramaters in respect to form, substance, or degree of difficulty.

Accordingly, acquaintance with, and practice in, the coding question is recommended for the serious candidate.

EXAMINATION SECTION
TEST 1

DIRECTIONS:

```
                              CODE TABLE
Name of Applicant    H A N G S B R U K E
Test Code            c o m p l e x i t y
File Number          0 1 2 3 4 5 6 7 8 9
```

Assume that each of the above *capital letters* is the first letter of the Name of an Applicant, that the *small letter* directly beneath each capital letter is the Test Code for the Applicant, and that the *number* directly beneath each code letter is the File Number for the Applicant.
In each of the following questions, the test code letters and the file numbers in Columns 2 and 3 should correspond to the capital letters in Column 1. For each question, look at each column carefully and mark your answer as follows:

If there is an error only in Column 2, mark your answer A.
If there is an error only in Column 3, mark your answer B.
If there is an error in both Columns 2 and 3, mark your answer C.
If both Columns 2 and 3 are correct, mark your answer D.

The following sample question is given to help you understand the procedure.

SAMPLE QUESTION

Column 1	Column 2	Column 3
AKEHN	otyci	18902

2 (#1)

In Column 2, the final test code letter "i" should be "m." Column 3 is correctly coded to Column 1. Since there is an error only in Column 2, the answer is A

	Column 1	Column 2	Column 3	
1.	NEKKU	mytti	29987	1.__
2.	KRAEB	txlye	86095	2.__
3.	ENAUK	ymoit	92178	3.__
4.	REANA	xeomo	69121	4.__
5.	EKHSE	ytcxy	97049	5.__

KEY (CORRECT ANSWERS)

1. B
2. C
3. D
4. A
5. C

TEST 2

DIRECTIONS: The employee identification codes in Column I begin and end with a capital letter and have an eight-digit number in between. In Questions 1 through 8, employee identification codes in Column I are to be arranged according to the following rules:

First: Arrange in alphabetical order according to the first letter.

Second: When two or more employee identification codes have the same first letter, arrange in alphabetical order according to the last letter.

Third: When two or more employee codes have the same first and last letters, arrange in numerical order beginning with the lowest number.

The employee identification codes in Column I are numbered 1 through 5 in the order in which they are listed. In Column II the numbers 1 through 5 are arranged in four different ways to show different arrangements of the corresponding employee identification numbers. Choose the answer in Column II in which the employee identification numbers are arranged according to the above rules.

SAMPLE QUESTION

Column I	Column II
1. E75044127B	A. 4, 1, 3, 2, 5
2. B96399104A	B. 4, 1, 2, 3, 5
3. B93939086A	C. 4, 3, 2, 5, 1
4. B47064465H	D. 3, 2, 5, 4, 1
5. B99040922A	

In the sample question, the four employee identification codes starting with B should be put before the employee identification code starting with E. The employee identification codes starting with B and ending with A should be put before the employee identification codes starting with B and ending with H. The three employee identification codes starting with B and ending with A should be listed in numerical order, beginning with the lowest number. The correct way to arrange the employee identification codes, therefore, is 3, 2, 5, 4, 1 shown below.

3. B93939086A
2. B96399104A
5. B99040922A
4. B47064465H
1. E75044127B

Therefore, the answer to the sample question is D. Now answer the following questions according to the above rules.

Column I

1.
1. G42786441J
2. H45665413J
3. G43117690J
4. G43546698I
5. G41679942I

Column II

A. 2, 5, 4, 3, 1
B. 5, 4, 1, 3, 2
C. 4, 5, 1, 3, 2
D. 1, 3, 5, 4, 2

1._____

2 (#2)

2. 1. S44556178T   A. 1, 3, 5, 2, 4
    2. T43457169T   B. 4, 3, 5, 2, 1
    3. S53321176T   C. 5, 3, 1, 2, 4
    4. T53317998S   D. 5, 1, 3, 4, 2
    5. S67673942S

3. 1. R63394217D   A. 5, 4, 2, 3, 1
    2. R63931247D   B. 1, 5, 3, 2, 4
    3. R53931247D   C. 5, 3, 1, 2, 4
    4. R66874239D   D. 5, 1, 2, 3, 4
    4. R46799366D

4. 1. A35671968B   A. 3, 2, 1, 4, 5
    2. A35421794C   B. 2, 3, 1, 5, 4
    3. A35466987B   C. 1, 3, 2, 4, 5
    4. C10435779A   D. 3, 1, 2, 4, 5
    5. C00634779B

5. 1. I99746426Q   A. 2, 1, 3, 5, 4
    2. I10445311Q   B. 5, 4, 2, 1, 3
    3. J63749877P   C. 4, 5, 3, 2, 1
    4. J03421739Q   D. 2, 1, 4, 5, 3
    5. J00765311Q

6. 1. M33964217N   A. 4, 1, 5, 2, 3
    2. N33942770N   B. 5, 1, 4, 3, 2
    3. N06155881M   C. 4, 1, 5, 3, 2
    4. M00433669M   D. 1, 4, 5, 2, 3
    5. M79034577N

7. 1. D77643905C   A. 1, 2, 5, 3, 4
    2. D44106788C   B. 5, 3, 2, 1, 4
    3. D13976022F   C. 2, 1, 5, 3, 4
    4. D97655430E   D. 2, 1, 4, 5, 3
    5. D00439776F

8. 1. W22746920A   A. 2, 1, 3, 4, 5
    2. W22743720A   B. 2, 1, 5, 3, 4
    3. W32987655A   C. 1, 2, 3, 4, 5
    4. W43298765A   D. 1, 2, 5, 3, 4
    5. W30987433A

KEY (CORRECT ANSWERS)

1. B   5. A
2. D   6. C
3. C   7. D
4. D   8. B

TEST 3

DIRECTIONS: Each of the following equations consists of three sets of names and name codes. In each question, the two names and name codes on the same line are supposed to be exactly the same.

Look carefully at each set of names and codes and mark your answer:
- A. if there are mistakes in all three sets
- B. if there are mistakes in two of the sets
- C. if there is a mistake in only one set
- D. if there are no mistakes in any of the sets

The following sample question is given to help you understand the procedure.

Macabe, John N.	- V	53162	Macade, John N.	- V	53162
Howard, Joan S.	- J	24791	Howard, Joan S.	- J	24791
Ware, Susan B.	- A	45068	Ware, Susan B.	- A	45968

In the above sample question, the names and name codes of the first set are not exactly the same because of the spelling of the last name (Macabe - Macade). The names and name codes of the second set are exactly the same. The names and name codes of the third set are not exactly the same because the two name codes are different (A 45068 - A 45968). Since there are mistakes in only 2 of the sets, the answer to the sample question is B.

1. Powell, Michael C. - 78537 F   Powell, Michael C. - 78537 F   1.____
   Martinez, Pablo, J. - 24435 P   Martinez, Pablo J. - 24435 P
   MacBane, Eliot M. - 98674 E   MacBane, Eliot M. - 98674 E

2. Fitz-Kramer Machines Inc. - 259090   Fitz-Kramer Machines Inc. - 259090   2.____
   Marvel Cleaning Service - 482657   Marvel Cleaning Service - 482657
   Donate, Carl G. - 637418   Danato, Carl G. - 687418

3. Martin Davison Trading Corp. - 43108 T   Martin Davidson Trading Corp. - 43108 T   3.____
   Cotwald Lighting Fixtures - 76065 L   Cotwald Lighting Fixtures - 70056 L
   R. Crawford Plumbers - 23157 C   R. Crawford Plumbers - 23157 G

4. Fraiman Engineering Corp. - M4773   Friaman Engineering Corp. -M4773   4.____
   Neuman, Walter B. - N7745   Neumen, Walter B. - N7745
   Pierce, Eric M. - W6304   Pierce, Eric M. - W6304

5. Constable, Eugene - B 64837   Comstable, Eugene - B 64837   5.____
   Derrick, Paul - H 27119   Derrik, Paul - H 27119
   Heller, Karen - S 49606   Heller, Karen - S 46906

6. Hernando Delivery Service Co. - D 7456   Hernando Delivery Service Co. - D 7456   6.____
   Barettz Electrical Supplies - N 5392   Barettz Electrical Supplies - N 5392
   Tanner, Abraham - M 4798   Tanner, Abraham - M 4798

7. Kalin Associates - R 38641   Kaline Associates - R 38641   7.____
   Sealey, Robert E. - P 63533   Sealey, Robert E. - P 63553
   Scalsi Office Furniture   Scalsi Office Furniture

2 (#3)

8. Janowsky, Philip M.- 742213 Janowsky, Philip M.- 742213 8.____
   Hansen, Thomas H. - 934816 Hanson, Thomas H. - 934816
   L. Lester and Son Inc. - 294568 L. Lester and Son Inc. - 294568

KEY (CORRECT ANSWERS)

1. D
2. C
3. A
4. B
5. A

6. D
7. B
8. C

TEST 4

DIRECTIONS: The following questions are to be answered on the basis of the following Code Table. In this table, for each number, a corresponding code letter is given. Each of the questions contains three pairs of numbers and code letters. In each pair, the code letters should correspond with the numbers in accordance with the Code Table.

CODE TABLE

Number	1	2	3	4	5	6	7	8	9	0
Corresponding Code Letter	Y	N	Z	X	W	T	U	P	S	R

In some of the pairs below, an error exists in the coding. Examine the pairs in each question carefully. If an error exists in:
- Only one of the pairs in the question, mark your answer A.
- Any two pairs in the question, mark your answer B.
- All three pairs in the question, mark your answer C.
- None of the pairs in the question, mark your answer D.

SAMPLE QUESTION

```
37258   -  ZUNWP
948764  -  SXPTTX
73196   -  UZYSP
```

In the above sample, the first pair is correct since each number, as listed, has the correct corresponding code letter. In the second pair, an error exists because the number 7 should have the code letter U instead of the letter T. In the third pair, an error exists because the number 6 should have the code letter T instead of the letter P. Since there are errors in two of the three pairs, the correct answer is B.

1. 493785   - XSZUPW
   86398207 - PTUSPNRU
   5943162   - WSXZYTN

2. 5413968412 - WXYZSTPXYR
   8763451297 - PUTZXWYZSU
   4781965302 - XUPYSUWZRN

3. 79137584 - USYRUWPX
   638247   - TZPNXS
   49679312 - XSTUSZYN

4. 37854296 - ZUPWXNST
   09183298 - RSYXZNSP
   91762358 - SYUTNXWP

5. 3918762485 - ZSYPUTNXPW
   1578291436 - YWUPNSYXZT
   2791385674 - NUSYZPWTUX

63

6. 197546821 - YSUWSTPNY   6.___
   873024867 - PUZRNWPTU
   583179246 - WPZYURNXT

7. 510782463 - WYRUSNXTZ   7.___
   478192356 - XUPYSNZWT
   961728532 - STYUNPWXN

KEY (CORRECT ANSWERS)

1. A
2. C
3. B
4. B
5. D

6. C
7. B

TEST 5

DIRECTIONS: Assume that each of the capital letters is the first letter of the name of a city using EAM equipment. The number directly beneath each capital letter is the code number for the city. The small letter beneath each code number is the code letter for the number of EAM divisions in the city and the + or - symbol directly beneath each code letter is the code symbol which signifies whether or not the city uses third generation computers with the EAM equipment.

The questions that follow show City Letters in Column I, Code Numbers in Column II, Code Letters in Column III, and Code Symbols in Column IV. If correct. each City Letter in Column I should correspond by position with each of the three codes shown in the other three columns, in accordance with the coding key shown. *BUT* there are some errors. For each question,

If there is a total of *ONE* error in Columns 2, 3, and 4, mark your answer A.
If there is a total of *TWO* errors in Columns 2, 3, and 4, mark your answer B.
If there is a total of *THREE* errors in Columns 2, 3, and 4, mark your answer C.
If Columns 2, 3, and 4 are correct, mark your answer D.

SAMPLE QUESTION

I	II	III	IV
City Letter	Code Numbers	Code Letters	Code Symbols
Y J M O S	5 3 7 9 8	e b g i h	- - + + -

The errors are as follows: In Column 2, the Code Number should be "2" instead of "3" for City Letter "J," and in Column 4 the Code Symbol should be "+" instead of "-" for City Letter "Y." Since there is a total of two errors in Columns 2, 3, and 4, the answer to this sample question is B.

Now answer questions 1 through 9 according to these rules.

CODING KEY

City Letter	P	J	R	T	Y	K	M	S	O
Code Number	1	2	3	4	5	6	7	8	9
Code Letter	a	b	c	d	e	f	g	h	i
Code Symbol	+	-	+	-	+	-	+	-	+

	I City Letters	II Code Numbers	III Code Letters	IV Code Symbols	
1.	K O R M P	6 9 3 7 1	f i e g a	- - + + +	1.____
2.	O T P S Y	9 4 1 8 6	b d a h e	+ - - - +	2.____
3.	R S J T M	3 8 1 4 7	c h b e g	- - - - +	3.____
4.	P M S K J	1 7 8 6 2	a g h f b	+ + - - -	4.____
5.	M Y T J R	7 5 4 2 3	g e d f c	+ + - - +	5.____
6.	T P K Y O	4 1 6 7 9	d a f e i	- + - + -	6.____
7.	S K O R T	8 6 9 3 5	h f i c d	- - + + -	7.____
8.	J R Y P K	2 3 5 1 9	b d e a f	- + + + -	8.____
9.	R O M P Y	4 9 7 1 5	c i g a d	+ + - + +	9.____

KEY (CORRECT ANSWERS)

1. B
2. C
3. C
4. D
5. A

6. B
7. A
8. B
9. C

TEST 6

Assume that each of the capital letters is the first letter of the name of an offense, that the small letter directly beneath each capital letter is the code letter for the offense, and that the number directly beneath each code letter is the file number for the offense.

DIRECTIONS: In each of the following questions, the code letters and file numbers should correspond to the capital letters.

If there is an error only in Column 2, mark your answer A.
If there is an error only in Column 3, mark your answer B.
If there is an error in both Column 2 and Column 3, mark your answer C.
If both Columns 2 and 3 are correct, mark your answer D.

SAMPLE QUESTION

Column 1	Column 2	Column 3
BNARGHSVVU	emoxtylcci	6357905118

The code letters in Column 2 are correct but the first "5" in Column 3 should be "2." Therefore, the answer is B. Now answer the following questions according to the above rules.

CODE TABLE

Name of Offense	V	A	N	D	S	B	R	U	G	H
Code Letter	c	o	m	p	l	e	x	i	t	y
File Number	1	2	3	4	5	6	7	8	9	0

	Column 1	Column 2	Column 3	
1.	HGDSBNBSVR	ytplxmelcx	0945736517	1.____
2.	SDGUUNHVAH	lptiimycoy	5498830120	2.____
3.	BRSNAAVUDU	exlmooctpi	6753221848	3.____
4.	VSRUDNADUS	cleipmopil	1568432485	4.____
5.	NDSHVRBUAG	mplycxeiot	3450175829	5.____
6.	GHUSNVBRDA	tyilmcexpo	9085316742	6.____
7.	DBSHVURANG	pesycixomt	4650187239	7.____
8.	RHNNASBDGU	xymnolepti	7033256398	8.____

KEY (CORRECT ANSWERS)

1. C
2. D
3. A
4. C
5. B

6. D
7. A
8. C

TEST 7

DIRECTIONS: Each of the following questions contains three sets of code letters and code numbers. In each set, the code numbers should correspond with the code letters as given in the Table, but there is a coding error in some of the sets. Examine the sets in each question carefully.

Mark your answer A if there is a coding error in only ONE of the sets in the question.
Mark your answer B if there is a coding error in any TWO of the sets in the question.
Mark your answer C if there is a coding error in all THREE sets in the question.
Mark your answer D if there is a coding error in NONE of the sets in the question.

SAMPLE QUESTION

fgzduwaf - 35720843
uabsdgfw - 04262538
hhfaudgs - 99340257

In the above sample question, the first set is right because each code number matches the code letter as in the Code Table. In the second set, the corresponding number for the code letter b is wrong because it should be 1 instead of 2. In the third set, the corresponding number for the last code letter s is wrong because it should be 6 instead of 7. Since there is an error in two of the sets, the answer to the above sample question is B.

In the Code Table below, each code letter has a corresponding code number directly beneath it.

CODE TABLE

Code Letter	b	d	f	a	g	s	z	w	h	u
Code Number	1	2	3	4	5	6	7	8	9	0

1. fsbughwz - 36104987   zwubgasz - 78025467   1._____
   ghgufddb - 59583221

2. hafgdaas - 94351446   ddsfabsd - 22734162   2._____
   wgdbssgf - 85216553

3. abfbssbd - 41316712   ghzfaubs - 59734017   3._____
   sdbzfwza - 62173874

4. whfbdzag - 89412745   daaszuub - 24467001   4._____
   uzhfwssd - 07936623

5. zbadgbuh - 71425109   dzadbbsz - 27421167   5._____
   gazhwaff - 54798433

6. fbfuadsh - 31304265   gzfuwzsb - 57300671   6._____
   bashhgag - 14699535

69

KEY (CORRECT ANSWERS)

1. B
2. C
3. B
4. B
5. D
6. C

TEST 8

DIRECTIONS: The following questions are to be answered on the basis of the following Code Table. In this table every letter has a corresponding code number to be punched. Each question contains three pairs of letters and code numbers. In each pair, the code numbers should correspond with the letters in accordance with the Code Table.

CODE TABLE

Letter	P	L	A	N	D	C	O	B	U	R
Corresponding Code Number	1	2	3	4	5	6	7	8	9	0

In some of the pairs below, an error exists in the coding. Examine the pairs in each question. Mark your answer

    A if there is a mistake in only *one* of the pairs
    B if there is a mistake in only *two* of the pairs
    C if there is a mistake in *all three* of the pairs
    D if there is a mistake in *none* of the pairs

SAMPLE QUESTION

    LCBPUPAB - 26819138
    ACOABOL - 3683872
    NDURONUC - 46901496

In the above sample, the first pair is correct since each letter as listed has the correct corresponding code number. In the second pair, an error exists because the letter O should have the code number 7, instead of 8. In the third pair, an error exists because the letter D should have the code number 5, instead of 6. Since there are errors in two of the three pairs, your answer should be B.

1. ADCANPLC - 35635126 DORURBBO - 57090877 1._____
 PNACBUCP - 14368061

2. LCOBLRAP - 26782931 UPANUPCD - 91349156 2._____
 RLDACLRO - 02536207

3. LCOROPAR - 26707130 BALANRUP - 83234091 3._____
 DOPOAULL - 57173922

4. ONCRUBAP - 74609831 DCLANORD - 56243705 4._____
 AORPDUR - 3771590

5. PANRBUCD - 13408965 UAOCDPLR - 93765120 5._____
 OPDDOBRA - 71556803

6. BAROLDCP - 83072561 PNOCOBLA - 14767823 6._____
 BURPDOLA - 89015723

7. ANNCPABO - 34461387 DBALDRCP - 58325061 7._____
 ACRPOUL - 3601792

2 (#8)

8. BLAPOUR - 8321790　　　NOACNPL - 4736412　　　　8.____
   RODACORD - 07536805

9. ADUBURCL - 3598062　　　NOCOBAPR - 47578310　　　9.____
   PRONDALU - 10754329

10. UBADCLOR - 98356270　　　NBUPPARA - 48911033　　　10.____
    LONDUPRC - 27459106

KEY (CORRECT ANSWERS)

1. C
2. B
3. D
4. B
5. A

6. D
7. B
8. B
9. C
10. A

TEST 9

DIRECTIONS: Answer questions 1 through 10 ONLY on the basis of the following information.

Column I consists of serial numbers of dollar bills. Column II shows different ways of arranging the corresponding serial numbers.

The serial numbers of dollar bills in Column I begin and end with a capital letter and have an eight-digit number in between. The serial numbers in Column I are to be arranged according to the following rules:

FIRST: In alphabetical order according to the first letter.

SECOND: When two or more serial numbers have the same first letter, in alphabetical order according to the last letter.

THIRD: When two or more serial numbers have the same first and last letters, in numerical order, beginning with the lowest number.

The serial numbers in Column I are numbered (1) through (5) in the order in which they are listed. In Column II the numbers (1) through (5) are arranged in four different ways to show different arrangements of the corresponding serial numbers. Choose the answer in Column II in which the serial numbers are arranged according to the above rules.

SAMPLE QUESTION

	COLUMN I		COLUMN II
(1)	E75044127B	(A)	4, 1, 3, 2, 5
(2)	B96399104A	(B)	4, 1, 2, 3, 5
(3)	B93939086A	(C)	4, 3, 2, 5, 1
(4)	B47064465H	(D)	3, 2, 5, 4, 1
(5)	B99040922A		

In the sample question, the four serial numbers starting with B should be put before the serial number starting with E. The serial numbers starting with B and ending with A should be put before the serial number starting with B and ending with H. The three serial numbers starting with B and ending with A should be listed in numerical order, beginning with the lowest number. The correct way to arrange the serial numbers, therefore, is:

(3) B93939086A
(2) B96399104A
(5) B99040922A
(4) B47064465H
(1) E75044127B

Since the order of arrangement is 3, 2, 5, 4, 1, the answer to the sample question is (D).

	COLUMN I		COLUMN II
1. (1)	P44343314Y	A.	2, 3, 1, 4, 5
(2)	P44141341S	B.	1, 5, 3, 2, 4
(3)	P44141431L	C.	4, 2, 3, 5, 1
(4)	P41143413W	D.	5, 3, 2, 4, 1
(5)	P44313433H		
2. (1)	D89077275M	A.	3, 2, 5, 4, 1
(2)	D98073724N	B.	1, 4, 3, 2, 5
(3)	D90877274N	C.	4, 1, 5, 2, 3
(4)	D98877275M	D.	1, 3, 2, 5, 4
(5)	D98873725N		

3.	(1)	H32548137E		A.	2,	4,	5,	1,	3
	(2)	H35243178A		B.	1,	5,	2,	3,	4
	(3)	H35284378F		C.	1,	5,	2,	4,	3
	(4)	H35288337A		D.	2,	1,	5,	3,	4
	(5)	H32883173B							
4.	(1)	K24165039H		A.	4,	2,	5,	3,	1
	(2)	F24106599A		B.	2,	3,	4,	1,	5
	(3)	L21406639G		C.	4,	2,	5,	1,	3
	(4)	C24156093A		D.	1,	3,	4,	5,	2
	(5)	K24165593D							
5.	(1)	H79110642E		A.	2,	1,	3,	5,	4
	(2)	H79101928E		B.	2,	1,	4,	5,	3
	(3)	A79111567F		C.	3,	5,	2,	1,	4
	(4)	H79111796E		D.	4,	3,	5,	1,	2
	(5)	A79111618F							
6.	(1)	P16388385W		A.	3,	4,	5,	2,	1
	(2)	R16388335V		B.	2,	3,	4,	5,	1
	(3)	P16383835W		C.	2,	4,	3,	1,	5
	(4)	R18386865V		D.	3,	1,	5,	2,	4
	(5)	P18686865W							
7.	(1)	B42271749G		A.	4,	1,	5,	2,	3
	(2)	B42271779G		B.	4,	1,	2,	5,	3
	(3)	E43217779G		C.	1,	2,	4,	5,	3
	(4)	B42874119C		D.	5,	3,	1,	2,	4
	(5)	E42817749G							
8.	(1)	M57906455S		A.	4,	1,	5,	3,	2
	(2)	N87077758S		B.	3,	4,	1,	5,	2
	(3)	N87707757B		C.	4,	1,	5,	2,	3
	(4)	M57877759B		D.	1,	5,	3,	2,	4
	(5)	M57906555S							
9.	(1)	C69336894Y		A.	2,	5,	3,	1,	4
	(2)	C69336684V		B.	3,	2,	5,	1,	4
	(3)	C69366887W		C.	3,	1,	4,	5,	2
	(4)	C69366994Y		D.	2,	5,	1,	3,	4
	(5)	C69336865V							
10.	(1)	A56247181D		A.	1,	5,	3,	2,	4
	(2)	A56272128P		B.	3,	1,	5,	2,	4
	(3)	H56247128D		C.	3,	2,	1,	5,	4
	(4)	H56272288P		D.	1,	5,	2,	3,	4
	(5)	A56247188D							

KEY (CORRECT ANSWERS)

1.	D	6.	D
2.	B	7.	B
3.	A	8.	A
4.	C	9.	A
5.	C	10.	D

TEST 10

DIRECTIONS: Answer the following questions on the basis of the instructions, the code, and the sample questions given below. Assume that an officer at a certain location is equipped with a two-way radio to keep him in constant touch with his security headquarters. Radio messages and replies are given in code form, as follows:

CODE TABLE

Radio Code for Situation	J	P	M	F	B
Radio Code for Action to be Taken	o	r	a	z	q
Radio Response for Action Being Taken	1	2	3	4	5

Assume that each of the above capital letters is the radio code for a particular type of situation, that the small letter below each capital letter is the radio code for the action an officer is directed to take, and that the number directly below each small letter is the radio response an officer should make to indicate what action was actually taken.

In each of the following questions, the code letter for the action directed (Column 2) and the code number for the action taken (Column 3) should correspond to the capital letters in Column 1.

INSTRUCTIONS:
If only Column 2 is different from Column 1, mark your answer I.
If only Column 3 is different from Column 1, mark your answer II.
If both Column 2 and Column 3 are different from Column I, mark your answer III.
If both Columns 2 and 3 are the same as Column 1, mark your answer IV.

SAMPLE QUESTION

Column 1	Column 2	Column 3
JPFMB	orzaq	12453

The CORRECT answer is: A. I B. II C. III D. IV
The code letters in Column 2 are correct, but the numbers "53" in Column 3 should be "35." Therefore, the answer is B. Now answe the following questions according to the above rules.

	Column 1	Column 2	Column 3	
1.	PBFJM	rqzoa	25413	1.____
2.	MPFBJ	zrqao	32541	2.____
3.	JBFPM	oqzra	15432	3.____
4.	BJPMF	qaroz	51234	4.____
5.	PJFMB	rozaq	21435	5.____
6.	FJBMP	zoqra	41532	6.____

KEY (CORRECT ANSWERS)

1. D
2. C
3. B
4. A
5. D
6. A

NAME AND NUMBER CHECKING

EXAMINATION SECTION
TEST 1

DIRECTIONS: This test is designed to measure your speed and accuracy. You are urged to work both quickly and accurately and to do correctly as many lists as you can in the time allowed. The test consists of lists of pairs of names and numbers. Count the number of IDENTICAL pairs in each list. Then, select the correct number, 1, 2, 3, 4, or 5, and indicate your choice by circling the corresponding number on your answer paper, Two sample questions are presented for your guidance, together with the correct solutions.

SAMPLE QUESTIONS

SAMPLE LIST A

		CIRCLE CORRECT ANSWER
Adelphi College	- Adelphia College	1 2 3 4 5
Braxton Corp.	- Braxeton Corp.	
Wassaic State School	- Wassaic State School	
Central Islip State Hospital	- Central Isllip State	
Greenwich House	- Greenwich House	

NOTE that there are only two correct pairs - Wassaic State School and Greenwich House. Therefore, the CORRECT answer is 2.

SAMPLE LIST B

78453694	- 78453684	1 2 3 4 5
784530	- 784530	
533	- 534	
67845	- 67845	
2368745	- 2368755	

NOTE that there are only two correct pairs - 784530 and 67845. Therefore, the CORRECT answer is 2.

LIST 1

98654327	- 98654327	1 2 3 4 5
74932564	- 74922564	
61438652	- 61438652	
01297653	- 01287653	
1865439765	- 1865439765	

LIST 2

478362	- 478363	1 2 3 4 5
278354792	- 278354772	
9327	- 9327	
297384625	- 27384625	
6428156	- 6428158	

2 (#1)

                                                                      CIRCLE
                                                  CORRECT ANSWER

LIST 3
   Abbey House   - Abbey House   1 2 3 4 5
   Actors' Fund Home   - Actor's Fund Home
   Adrian Memorial   - Adrian Memorial
   A. Clayton Powell Home   - Clayton Powell House
   Abott E. Kittredge Club   - Abbott E. Kitteredge Club

LIST 4
   3682   - 3692   1 2 3 4 5
   21937453829   - 31937453829
   723   - 733
   2763920   - 2763920
   47293   - 47293

LIST 5
   Adra House   - Adra House   1 2 3 4 5
   Adolescents' Court   - Adolescents' Court
   Cliff Villa   - Cliff Villa
   Clark Neighborhood House - Clark Neighborhood House
   Alma Mathews House   - Alma Mathews House

LIST 6
   28734291   - 28734271   1 2 3 4 5
   63810263849   - 63810263846
   26831027   - 26831027
   368291   - 368291
   7238102637   - 7238102637

LIST 7
   Albion State T.S.   - Albion State T.C.   1 2 3 4 5
   Clara de Hirsch Home - Clara De Hirsch Home
   Alice Carrington Royce - Alice Carington Royce
   Alice Chopin Nursery - Alice Chapin Nursery
   Lighthouse Eye Clinic - Lighthouse Eye Clinic

LIST 8
   327   - 329   1 2 3 4 5
   712438291026   - 712438291026
   2753829142   - 275382942
   826287   - 826289
   26435162839   - 26435162839

LIST 9
   Letchworth Village - Letchworth Village   1 2 3 4 5
   A.A.A.E. Inc.   - A.A.A.E. Inc.
   Clear Pool Camp   - Clear Pool Camp
   A.M.M.L.A. Inc.   - A.M.M.L.A. Inc.
   J.G. Harbard   - J.G. Harbord

3 (#1)

		CIRCLE CORRECT ANSWER

LIST 10
    8254   - 8256   1   2   3   4   5
    2641526   - 2641526
    4126389012   - 4126389102
    725   - 725
    76253917287   - 76253917287

LIST 11
    Attica State Prison   - Attica State Prison   1   2   3   4   5
    Nellie Murrah   - Nellie Murrah
    Club Marshall   - Club Marshal
    Assissium Casea-Maria   - Assissium Casa-Maria
    The Homestead   - The Homestead

LIST 12
    2691   - 2691   1   2   3   4   5
    623819253627   - 623819253629
    28637   - 28937
    278392736   - 278392736
    52739   - 52739

LIST 13
    A.I.C.P. Boys Camp   - A.I.C.P. Boy's Camp   1   2   3   4   5
    Einar Chrystie   - Einar Christyie
    Astoria Center   - Astoria Center
    G. Frederick Brown   - G. Federick Browne
    Vacation Service   - Vacation Services

LIST 14
    728352689   - 728352688   1   2   3   4   5
    643728   - 643728
    37829176   - 37827196
    8425367   - 8425369
    65382018   - 65382018

LIST 15
    E.S. Streim   - E.S. Strim   1   2   3   4   5
    Charles E. Higgins   - Charles E. Higgins
    Baluvelt, N.Y.   - Blauwelt, N.Y.
    Roberta Magdalen   - Roberto Magdalen
    Ballard School   - Ballard School

LIST 16
    7382   - 7392   1   2   3   4   5
    281374538299   - 291374538299
    623   - 633
    6273730   - 6273730
    63392   - 63392

4 (#1)

CIECLE
CORRECT ANSWER

LIST 17
    Orrin Otis   - Orrin Otis   1 2 3 4 5
    Barat Settlement   - Barat Settlemen
    Emmanuel House   - Emmanuel House
    William T. McCreery - William T. McCreery
    Seamen's Home   - Seaman's Home

LIST 18
    72824391   - 72834371   1 2 3 4 5
    3729106237   - 37291106237
    82620163849   - 82620163846
    37638921   - 37638921
    82631027   - 82631027

LIST 19
    Commonwealth Fund   - Commonwealth Fund   1 2 3 4 5
    Anne Johnsen   - Anne Johnson
    Bide-a-Wee Home   - Bide-a-Wee Home
    Riverdale-on-Hudson   - Riverdal-on-Hudson
    Bialystoker Home   - Bailystoker Home

LIST 20
    9271   - 9271   1 2 3 4 5
    392918352627   - 392018852629
    72637   - 72637
    927392736   - 927392736
    92739   - 92739

LIST 21
    Charles M. Stump   - Charles M. Stump   1 2 3 4 5
    Bourne Workshop   - Buorne Workshop
    B'nai Bi'rith   - B'nai Brith
    Poppenhuesen Institute   - Poppenheusen Institute
    Consular Service   - Consular Service

LIST 22
    927352689   - 927352688   1 2 3 4 5
    647382   - 648382
    93729176   - 93727196
    649536718   - 649536718
    5835367   - 5835369

LIST 23
    L.S. Bestend   - L.S. Bestent   1 2 3 4 5
    Hirsch Mfg. Co.   - Hircsh Mfg. Co.
    F.H. Storrs   - F.P. Storrs
    Camp Wassaic   - Camp Wassaic
    George Ballingham   - George Ballingham

5 (#1)

LIST 24
- 372846392048 — - 372846392048
- 334 — - 334
- 7283524678 — - 7283524678
- 7283 — - 7283
- 7283629372 — - 7283629372

LIST 25
- Dr. Stiles Company — - Dr. Stills Company
- Frances Hunsdon — - Frances Hunsdon
- Northrop Barrert — - Nothrup Barrent
- J. D. Brunjes — - J. D. Brunjes
- Theo. Claudel & Co. — - Theo. Claudel co.

CIRCLE CORRECT ANSWER
1 2 3 4 5

1 2 3 4 5

KEY (CORRECT ANSWERS)

1. 3
2. 1
3. 2
4. 2
5. 5

6. 3
7. 1
8. 2
9. 4
10. 3

11. 3
12. 3
13. 1
14. 2
15. 2

16. 2
17. 3
18. 2
19. 2
20. 4

21. 2
22. 1
23. 2
24. 5
25. 2

TEST 2

DIRECTIONS: This test is designed to measure your speed and accuracy. You are urged to work both quickly and accurately and to do correctly as many lists as you can in the time allowed. The test consists of lists of pairs of names and numbers. Count the number of IDENTICAL pairs in each list. Then, select the correct number, 1, 2, 3, 4, or 5, and indicate your choice by circling the corresponding number on your answer paper, Two sample questions are presented for your guidance, together with the correct solutions.

LIST 1
82728	- 82738	CIRCLE
82736292637	- 82736292639	CORRECT ANSWER
728	- 738	1 2 3 4 5
83926192527	- 83726192529	
82736272	- 82736272	

LIST 2
L. Pietri	- L. Pietri	
Mathewson, L.F.	- Mathewson, L.F.	
Funk & Wagnall	- Funk &. Wagnalls	1 2 3 4 5
Shimizu, Sojio	- Shimizu, Sojio	
Filing Equipment Bureau	- Filing Equipment Buraeu	

LIST 3
63801829374	- 63801839474	
283577657	- 283577657	
65689	- 65689	1 2 3 4 5
3457892026	- 3547893026	
2779	- 2778	

LIST 4
August Caille	- August Caille	
The Well-Fare Service	- The Wel-Fare Service	
K.L.M. Process Co.	- R.L.M. Process Co.	1 2 3 4 5
Merrill Littell	- Merrill Littell	
Dodd & Sons	- Dodd & Son	

LIST 5
998745732	- 998745733	
723	- 723	
463849102983	- 463849102983	1 2 3 4 5
8570	- 8570	
279012	- 279012	

LIST 6
M. A. Wender	- M.A. Winder	
Minneapolis Supply Co.	- Minneapolis Supply Co.	
Beverly Hills Corp	- Beverley Hills Corp.	1 2 3 4 5
Trafalgar Square	- Trafalgar Square	
Phifer, D.T.	- Phiefer, D.T.	

2 (#2)

CIRCLE
CORRECT ANSWER

LIST 7
7834629   - 7834629
3549806746   - 3549806746
97802564   - 97892564
689246   - 688246
2578024683   - 2578024683

1 2 3 4 5

LIST 8
Scadrons'   - Scadrons'
Gensen & Bro.   - Genson & Bro.
Firestone Co.   - Firestone Co.
H.L. Eklund   - H.L. Eklund
Oleomargarine Co.   - Oleomargarine Co.

1 2 3 4 5

LIST 9
782039485618   - 782039485618
53829172639   - 63829172639
892   - 892
82937482   - 829374820
52937456   - 53937456

1 2 3 4 5

LIST 10
First Nat'l Bank   - First Nat'l Bank
Sedgwick Machine Works   - Sedgewick Machine Works
Hectographia Co.   - Hectographia Corp.
Levet Bros.   - Levet Bros.
Multistamp Co.,Inc.   - Multistamp Co.,Inc.

1 2 3 4 5

LIST 11
7293   - 7293
6382910293   - 6382910292
981928374012   - 981928374912
58293   - 58393
18203649271   - 283019283745

1 2 3 4 5

LIST 12
Lowrey Lb'r Co.   - Lowrey Lb'r Co.
Fidelity Service - Fidelity Service
Reumann, J.A.   - Reumann, J.A.
Duophoto Ltd.   - Duophotos Ltd.
John Jarratt   - John Jaratt

1 2 3 4 5

LIST 13
6820384   - 6820384
383019283745   - 383019283745
63927102   - 63928102
91029354829   - 91029354829
58291728   - 58291728

1 2 3 4 5

83

3 (#2)

                                                                                     CIRCLE
                                                                                     CORRECT ANSWER

LIST 14
    Standard Press Co.   - Standard Press Co.   1 2 3 4 5
    Reliant Mf'g. Co.   - Relant Mf'g Co.
    M.C. Lynn   - M.C. Lynn
    J. Fredericks Company - G. Fredericks Company
    Wandermann, B.S.   - Wanderman, B.S.

LIST 15
    4283910293   - 4283010203   1 2 3 4 5
    992018273648   - 992018273848
    620   - 629
    752937273   - 752937373
    5392   - 5392

LIST 16
    Waldorf Hotel   - Waldorf Hotel   1 2 3 4 5
    Aaron Machinery Co.   - Aaron Machinery Co.
    Caroline Ann Locke   - Caroline Anne Locke
    McCabe Mfg. Co.   - McCabe Mfg. Co.
    R.L. Landres   - R.L. Landers

LIST 17
    68391028364   - 68391028394   1 2 3 4 5
    68293   - 68293
    739201   - 739201
    72839201   - 72839211
    739917   - 739719

LIST 18
    Balsam M.M.   - Balsamm, M.M.   1 2 3 4 5
    Steinway & Co.   - Stienway & M. Co.
    Eugene Elliott   - Eugene A. Elliott
    Leonard Loan Co.   - Leonard Loan Co.
    Frederick Morgan   - Frederick Morgen

LIST 19
    8929   - 9820   1 2 3 4 5
    392836472829   - 392836472829
    462   - 462 2039271
    827   - 2039276837
    53829   - 54829

LIST 20
    Danielson's Hofbrau - Danielson's Hafbrau   1 2 3 4 5
    Edward A. Truarme - Edward A. Truame
    Insulite Co.   - Insulite Co.
    Reisler Shoe Corp,   - Rielser Shoe Corp.
    L.L. Thompson   - L.L. Thompson

LIST 21
92839102837	- 92839102837
58891028	- 58891028
7291728	- 7291928
272839102839	- 272839102839
428192	- 428102

LIST 22
K.L. Veiller	- K.L. Veiller
Webster, Roy	- Webster, Ray
Drasner Spring Co.	- Drasner Spring Co.
Edward J. Cravenport	- Edward J. Cravanport
Harold Field	- Harold A. Field

LIST 23
2293	- 2293
4283910293	- 5382910292
871928374012	- 871928374912
68293	- 68393
8120364927	- 81293649271

LIST 24
Tappe, Inc	- Tappe, Inc.
A.M. Wentingworth	- A.M. Wentinworth
Scott A. Elliott	- Scott A. Elliott
Echeverria Corp.	- Echeverria Corp.
Bradford Victor Company	- Bradford Victer Company

LIST 25
4820384	- 4820384
393019283745	- 283919283745
63927102	- 63927102
91029354829	- 91029354829
48291728	- 48291728

CIRCLE CORRECT ANSWER

1 2 3 4 5

1 2 3 4 5

1 2 3 4 5

1 2 3 4 5

1 2 3 4 5

5 (#2)

KEY (CORRECT ANSWERS)

1.	1	11.	1
2.	3	12.	3
3.	2	13.	4
4.	2	14.	2
5.	4	15.	1
6.	2	16.	3
7.	3	17.	2
8.	4	18.	1
9.	2	19.	1
10.	3	20.	2

21.	3
22.	2
23.	1
24.	2
25.	4

ARITHMETICAL REASONING
EXAMINATION SECTION
TEST 1

DIRECTIONS: Each question or incomplete statement is followed by several suggested answers or completions. Select the one that BEST answers the question or completes the statement. *PRINT THE LETTER OF THE CORRECT ANSWER IN THE SPACE AT THE RIGHT.*

1. Liquid toilet soap is supplied in 5-gallon cans. If each of the twelve toilet rooms in your building uses an average of one quart of toilet soap per month, the amount of cans you should be required to requisite to cover needs for a three month period is

    A. two B. three C. four D. five

    1.____

2. A corridor is ten feet wide and 210 feet long. If it takes a two-man crew about one hour to mop 5,000 square feet, the amount of time required for mopping the corridor is MOST NEARLY _____ minutes.

    A. 30
    C. 15
    B. 25
    D. 10

    2.____

3. If 75 crates of food were ordered and 100 crates were delivered, then the shipment is larger than the number ordered by _____ crates.

    A. 10 B. 15 C. 25 D. 35

    3.____

4. If 200 boxes of merchandise were ordered and 100 boxes are delivered, then the shipment is short by _____ boxes.

    A. 50 B. 100 C. 150 D. 175

    4.____

5. You are to load a hand truck with cartons weighing a total of 200 pounds.
   If each carton weighs 20 pounds, then the TOTAL number of cartons to be loaded is

    A. 8 B. 9 C. 10 D. 11

    5.____

6. You are to unpack twelve cartons of paper and place the paper on a storage shelf.
   If each carton has eight packs of paper, then the number of packs of paper that you will place on the shelf is

    A. 72 B. 84 C. 96 D. 108

    6.____

7. If floor wax costs $2.90 a gallon, then the TOTAL cost of a carton in which there are six gallons of wax is

    A. $17.40 B. $19.00 C. $21.40 D. $29.00

    7.____

8. You know that a storage shelf unit can safely hold items up to a total weight of 300 pounds.
   If there are already 8 boxes of canned food on the shelves of the unit, all exactly the same, and each box weighs 25 pounds, then the number of the same boxes of canned food that you can safely add to those on the shelves is

    A. 4 B. 5 C. 6 D. 7

    8.____

2 (#1)

9. During the month of June, 40,587 people attended a city-owned swimming pool. In July, 13,014 more people attended the swimming pool than the number that had attended in June. In August, 39,655 people attended the swimming pool. The TOTAL number of people who attended the swimming pool during the months of June, July, and August was

   A. 80,242   B. 93,256   C. 133,843   D. 210,382

   9.____

10. Assume that your agency has been given $2,025 to purchase file cabinets.
    If each file cabinet costs $135, how many file cabinets can your agency purchase?

    A. 8   B. 10   C. 15   D. 16

    10.____

11. Assume that your unit ordered 14 staplers at a total cost of $30.20, and each stapler cost the same.
    The cost of one stapler was MOST NEARLY

    A. $1.02   B. $1.61   C. $2.16   D. $2.26

    11.____

12. Assume that you are responsible for counting and recording licensing fees collected by your department. On a particular day, your department collected in fees 40 checks in the amount of $6 each, 80 checks in the amount of $4 each, 45 twenty dollar bills, 30 ten dollar bills, 42 five dollar bills, and 186 one dollar bills.
    The TOTAL amount in fees collected on that day was

    A. $1,406   B. $1,706   C. $2,156   D. $2,356

    12.____

13. Assume that you are responsible for your agency's petty cash fund. During the month of February, you pay out 7 subway fares at 50¢ each and one taxi fare for $2.85. You pay out nothing else from the fund. At the end of February, you count the money left in the fund and find 3 one dollar bills, 4 quarters, 5 dimes, and 4 nickels. The amount of money you had available in the petty cash fund at the BEGINNING of February was

    A. $4.70   B. $6.35   C. $7.55   D. $11.05

    13.____

14. Assume that you are assigned to sell tickets at a city-owned ice skating rink. An adult ticket costs $1.50, and a children's ticket costs $.75. At the end of a day, you find that you have sold 36 adult tickets and 80 children's tickets.
    The TOTAL amount of money you collected for that day was

    A. $81.60   B. $106.00   C. $114.00   D. $116.00

    14.____

15. If each office worker files 487 index cards in one hour, how many cards can 26 office workers file in one hour?

    A. 10,662   B. 12,175   C. 12,662   D. 14,266

    15.____

16. Assume a city agency has 775 office workers.
    If 2 out of 25 office workers were absent on a particular day, how many office workers reported to work on that day?

    A. 713   B. 744   C. 750   D. 773

    16.____

17. If a worker earns $9.18 per hour and works a 40-hour week, his weekly pay will be

    A. $357.20   B. $366.20   C. $366.40   D. $367.20

    17.____

18. If a stock clerk earns $13.12 per hour and works a 40-hour week, how much will she receive in two weeks? 18.____

   A. $1,049.60 B. $1,049.80
   C. $1,050.60 D. $1,051.60

19. A stock clerk earns $9.18 per hour when he works a 40-hour week and is paid for overtime at time and a half for all time worked over 40 hours. 19.____
   How much money for overtime should he receive if he worked a 48-hour week?

   A. $109.16 B. $109.28 C. $110.16 D. $110.36

20. The reorder quantity is reached by multiplying the average monthly usage by the lead time (in months) and adding the minimum balance. For a particular item, the lead time is 2 months, the minimum balance is 100, and the average monthly usage is 150. 20.____
   The reorder quantity for this item is

   A. 300 B. 400 C. 600 D. 1,000

21. If a job can be completed by 4 employees in 6 days, how many days will it take 6 employees working at an equal speed to do the same job? 21.____

   A. 2 B. 3 C. 3 1/2 D. 4

22. If your rate of pay is $8.00 an hour for a 40-hour work week, and in an emergency you volunteer to work your half-hour lunch period for 5 days at straight time, what will your TOTAL gross pay be at the end of the week? 22.____

   A. $340 B. $350 C. $370 D. $380

23. If the gross weight of a trailer truck with a load of ferrous scrap removed from your storage yard is 67,130 pounds and the tare weight is 24,570 pounds, what is the weight, in gross tons, of the scrap removed? 23.____

   A. 17 B. 18 C. 19 D. 21

24. You receive a requisition for 2 1/2 gross of machine screws. The number of machine screws you should dispense is 24.____

   A. 300 B. 324 C. 360 D. 400

25. A requisition for a ream of paper is a request for how many sheets of paper? 25.____

   A. 200 B. 500 C. 750 D. 1,000

KEY (CORRECT ANSWERS)

1. A
2. B
3. C
4. B
5. C

6. C
7. A
8. A
9. C
10. C

11. C
12. C
13. D
14. C
15. C

16. A
17. D
18. A
19. C
20. B

21. D
22. A
23. D
24. C
25. B

SOLUTIONS TO PROBLEMS

1. (12)(1 qt.) = 12 qts. = 3 gallons per month. For 3 months, 9 gallons are needed. Since the soap is supplied in 5-gallon cans, 2 cans are required.

2. (10')(210') = 2100 sq.ft. Time required = (2100/5000) hrs. = .42 hrs. - 25 min. (Closest answer given is 30 min.)

3. 100 - 75 = 25 crates

4. 200 - 100 = 100 boxes

5. 200 20 = 10 cartons

6. (12) (8) = 96 packs of paper

7. ($2.90)(6) = $17.40

8. Maximum allowable number of boxes = 300 ÷ 25 = 12. Since there are already 8 boxes on the shelves, 4 more may be added.

9. Total number of people = 40,587 + 53,601 + 39,655 = 133,843

10. $2025 $135 = 15 file cabinets

11. $30.20 14 = $2.16 per stapler

12. (40)($6) + (80)($4) + (45)($20) + (30)($10) + (42)($5) + (186)($1) = $2156

13. (7)($.50) + (1)($2.85) + (3)($1) + (4)($.25) + (5)($.10) + (4)($.05) = $11.05

14. (36)($1.50) + (80)($.75) = $114.00

15. (26)(487) = 12,662 cards

16. 16. Since 23 out of 25 were present, this represents .92 of these workers. Then, (.92)(775) = 713

17. ($9.18)(40) = $367.20

18. ($13.12)(40)(2) = $1049.60

19. ($9.18)(40) + ($13.77)(8) = $477.36 total, but his overtime is (13.77)(8) = $110.16

20. Reorder quantity = (150)(2) + 100 = 400

21. (4)(6) = 24 employee-days. Then, 24 ÷ 6 = 4 days

22. ($8.00)(40) + ($8.00)(2.5) = $340

6 (#1)

23. 67,130 - 24,570 = 42,560 lbs. 2,000 = 21.28 tons = 21 tons

24. (2 1/2)(144) = 360 machine screws

25. 1 ream = 500 sheets of paper

———

TEST 2

DIRECTIONS: Each question or incomplete statement is followed by several suggested answers or completions. Select the one that BEST answers the question or completes the statement. *PRINT THE LETTER OF THE CORRECT ANSWER IN THE SPACE AT THE RIGHT.*

1. A bin in your storeroom measuring 2' x 1.5' x 4' has a storage volume of _____ cubic feet. 1._____

   A. 12   B. 24   C. 50   D. 72

2. A gill is equivalent to 8 fluid ounces. 2._____
   How many gills are required to fill a 5-gallon container with distilled water?

   A. 70   B. 75   C. 80   D. 85

3. A storage space 8'6" wide and 9'6" long has an area that is CLOSEST to _____ square feet. 3._____

   A. 80   B. 81   C. 82   D. 83

4. A drill bit has a diameter of 13/32 inch. 4._____
   Of the following, the decimal number CLOSEST to 13/32 is

   A. 0.406   B. 0.408   C. 0.410   D. 0.412

5. If repaired units come into your storeroom in a palletized container indicating that the gross weight is 2250 pounds, then the 5._____

   A. container alone weighs 2250 pounds
   B. repaired units alone weigh 2250 pounds
   C. repaired units and palletized container weigh 2250 pounds
   D. weight of 2250 pounds is approximate

6. You have 5 pieces of lumber. Their lengths are: 8'2", 6'4", 3'4", 5'9", and 4'5". 6._____
   What is the sum of the lengths of the 5 pieces of lumber?

   A. 26'   B. 26'9"   C. 27'10"   D. 28'

7. A full reel of 1,000 feet of power distribution cable weighs 8,095 pounds. The cable weighs 7.6 pounds per foot. The weight of the empty reel is _____ pounds. 7._____

   A. 465   B. 480   C. 495   D. 510

8. A crate 2' by 3' by 6' has a volume of _____ cubic yards. 8._____

   A. 6   B. 1 1/3   C. 18   D. 4

9. Of 600 pieces received in a shipment, 50 are inspected. Of the 50, 10 are found damaged. 9._____
   If the 50 are a representative sampling, the number of items in the entire shipment LIKELY to be damaged is

   A. 50   B. 60   C. 80   D. 120

10. A board having 3 square feet has how many square inches?   10._____

   A. 144   B. 288   C. 432   D. 576

11. A crate of material delivered to your storeroom has inscribed on it the words *Net Weight*   11._____
   250 pounds.
   This means that the

   A. weight of 250 pounds is approximate
   B. material and crate together weigh 250 pounds
   C. material alone weighs 250 pounds
   D. crate alone weighs 250 pounds

12. A box contains an equal number of brass and copper tubes. Each brass tube weighs 4   12._____
   pounds, each copper tube weighs 1 pound, and the empty box weighs 5 pounds. The
   total weight of the box and tubes is 200 pounds.
   The TOTAL number of tubes in the box is

   A. 39   B. 60   C. 78   D. 156

13. A caretaker received $70.00 for having worked from Monday through Friday, 9 M. to 5   13._____
   P.M., with one hour a day for lunch.
   The number of hours the caretaker would have to work to earn $12.00 is

   A. 10   B. 6
   C. 70 divided by 12   D. 70 minus 12

14. If the cost of a broom went up from $4.00 to $6.00, the percent INCREASE in the original   14._____
   cost is

   A. 20   B. 25   C. 33 1/3   D. 50

15. The AVERAGE of the numbers 3, 5, 7, 8, 12 is   15._____

   A. 5   B. 6   C. 7   D. 8

16. The cost of 100 bags of cotton cleaning cloths, 89 pounds per bag, at 7 cents per pound,   16._____
   is

   A. $549.35   B. $623.00   C. $700.00   D. $890.00

17. If 5 1/2 bags of sweeping compound cost $55.00, then 6 1/2 bags would cost   17._____

   A. $60.00   B. $62.50   C. $65.00   D. $67.00

18. The cost of cleaning supplies in a project averaged $330.00 a month during the first 8   18._____
   months of the year. How much can be spent each month for the last four months if the
   total amount that can be spent for cleaning supplies for the year is $3,880?

   A. $124.00   B. $220.00   C. $310.00   D. $330.00

19. A shelf in a supply closet can safely hold only 100 pounds. A package of paper towels   19._____
   weighs 2 pounds, a carton of disinfectant weighs 8 pounds, and a box of soap weighs 1
   pound. There are already 6 cartons of disinfectant and 6 boxes of soap on the shelf.
   How many packages of towels can be SAFELY placed there?

   A. 20   B. 23   C. 25   D. 27

20. A cleaning solution is made up of 4 gallons of water, 1 pint of liquid soap, and 1 pint of ammonia.
    How many gallons of water are needed to use up a gallon of ammonia?   20._____

    A. 8   B. 16   C. 24   D. 32

21. Suppose a caretaker has 50 stair halls to clean. If he cleans 74% of them, the number of stair halls still UNCLEANED is   21._____

    A. 38   B. 26   C. 24   D. 13

22. If a man has a 12 foot piece of wood and wishes to cut it into two pieces so that one piece is twice as long as the other, the LONGER piece should be _____ feet.   22._____

    A. 7   B. 7 1/2   C. 8   D. 8 1/2

23. If fuel oil costs $1.09 9/10 per gallon, and $224 was the total cost for a tank fill-up, how many gallons were delivered?   23._____

    A. 203.82   B. 190.59   C. 217.38   D. 179.97

24. A drill bit has a diameter of 17/36". Of the following, the decimal equivalent CLOSEST to 17/36 is   24._____

    A. 0.444   B. 0.531   C. 0.473   D. 0.472

25. If cleaning solution costs $1.53 per gallon, what is the TOTAL cost of 2 cartons of cleaning solution when each carton holds 12 one-gallon jugs?   25._____

    A. $36.24   B. $36.72   C. $39.12   D. $37.92

KEY (CORRECT ANSWERS)

1.	A	11.	C
2.	C	12.	C
3.	B	13.	B
4.	A	14.	D
5.	C	15.	C
6.	D	16.	B
7.	C	17.	C
8.	B	18.	C
9.	D	19.	B
10.	C	20.	D

21. D
22. C
23. A
24. D
25. B

SOLUTIONS TO PROBLEMS

1. Volume = (21)(1.5')(4') = 12 cu.ft.

2. 5 gallons = (128)(5) = 640 fluid oz. Then, 640 8 = 80 gills

3. Area = (8'6")(9'6") = (8.5')(9.5') = 80.75 = 81 sq.ft.

4. 13/32 = .40625 = .406

5. Gross weight = combined weight of repaired units and palletized container.

6. 8'2" + 6'4" + 3'4" + 5'9" + 4'5" = 26'24" = 28'

7. Empty reel weight = 8095 - (7.6)(1000) = 495 lbs.

8. (2')(3')(6') = 36 cu.ft. = 36/27 = 1 1/2 cu.yds.

9. 10/50 = 20%. Then, (20%)(600) = 120 are likely to be damaged.

10. 3 sq.ft. = (3)(144) = 432 sq.in.

11. Net weight refers to the contents of the crate, not including the crate's weight.

12. Let x = number of brass and copper tubes together. Then, $(1/2x)(4) + (1/2)(1) + 5 = 200$. Simplifying, we get $2.5x = 195$. Solving, $x = 78$

13. $70 is paid for (7)(5) = 35 hrs., which means $2 per hour. Thus, $12 is received in 12/2 = 6 hours.

14. Percent increase = ($2.00/$4.00)(100) = 50%

15. Average = (3+5+7+8+12)/5 = 35/5 = 7

16. Cost = (100)(89)($.07) = $623.00

17. $55 ÷ 5.5 = $10 per bag. Then, 6 1/2 bags cost (6 1/2)($10) = $65.00

18. Let x = amount spent during each of the last 4 months. Then, $(8)(\$330) + 4x = \$3880$. Solving, $x = \$310.00$

19. Let x = number of pkgs. of towels. Then, $2x + (6)(8) + (6)(1) = 100$. Simplifying, $2x = 46$. Solving, $x = 23$

20. Since 1 gallon = 8 pints, 1 gallon of ammonia requires (4)(8) = 32 gallons of water

21. Number of stair halls uncleaned = (.26)(50) = 13

22. Let x = longer piece, $1/2x$ = shorter piece. Then, $x + 1/2x = 12$. Solving, $x = 8$ ft.

6 (#2)

23. $224 ÷ $1.099 ≈ 203.82 gallons

24. 17/36 = .47$\overline{2}$ ≈ .472

25. Total cost = (2)(12)($1.53) = $36.72

TEST 3

DIRECTIONS: Each question or incomplete statement is followed by several suggested answers or completions. Select the one that BEST answers the question or completes the statement. *PRINT THE LETTER OF THE CORRECT ANSWER IN THE SPACE AT THE RIGHT.*

1. A storeroom is 100 feet long and 26 feet wide. One aisle 8 feet wide runs the length of the storeroom.
   One aisle 4 feet wide runs the width of the storeroom. If there were no other aisles, the number of square feet of usable storage space would be

   A. 1696 B. 1728 C. 2280 D. 2568

2. A discount of 1% is given on all purchases of a certain item In quantities of 100 units or more. An additional discount of 1% is given on that portion of the purchase which exceeds 300.
   If 450 units are purchased at a list price of $6.00, the total cost is

   A. $2,619 B. $2,664 C. $2,670 D. $2,682

3. The number of cartons measuring 3'x3'x2' which will be needed to pack 1,728 boxed Items each measuring 3"x9"x6" is

   A. 9 B. 18 C. 108 D. 192

4. A space 5 1/2 feet wide and 2 1/3 feet long has an area measured MOST NEARLY _____ square feet.

   A. 9 B. 10 C. 11 D. 12

5. One man is able to load two 2 1/2 ton trucks In one hour. To load ten such trucks, it will take ten men _____ hour(s).

   A. 1/2 B. 1 C. 2 D. 2 1/2

6. If the average height of the stacks In your section of the storehouse is 10', the area which will be occupied by 56,000 cubic feet of supplies, is MOST LIKELY to be

   A. 70'x80' B. 60'x90' C. 50'x60' D. 560'x100'

7. The number of cartons, each measuring two cubic feet, which can fit into a space which is 100 square feet in area and Is 8' high is

   A. 50 B. 200 C. 400 D. 800

8. When the floor area measures 200' by 200' and the maximum weight it can hold is 4,000 tons, then the safe floor load is _____ pounds per square foot.

   A. 20 B. 160 C. 200 D. 400

9. A carton 1' x 1' x 3' measures _____ cubic yard(s).

   A. 1/3 B. 1/9 C. 3 D. 9

10. You have received 6 cartons, each containing 60 boxes of staples, priced at $36.00 per carton.
    The price per box is

    A. $.10   B. $.60   C. $3.60   D. $6.00

11. The amount of space in cubic feet, required to store 100 boxes each, measuring 24" x 12" x 6", is

    A. 10   B. 100   C. 168   D. 1,008

12. Assume that it takes an average of 2 man-hours to stack 1 ton of certain supplies. In order to stack 30 tons, the number of men required to complete the job in ten hours is

    A. 6   B. 10   C. 15   D. 30

13. An area measures 20'x22 1/2'. The floor load is 100 lbs. per square foot.
    The total weight that can be stored in this area is MOST NEARLY _____ lbs.

    A. 450   B. 9,000   C. 22,500   D. 45,000

14. The price of a certain type of linoleum is $1.00 per square foot.
    The total cost of four pieces of 9'x12' linoleum is MOST NEARLY

    A. $105   B. $400   C. $430   D. $2,160

15. The number of board feet in a piece of lumber measuring 2" thick by 2' wide by 12' long is

    A. 12   B. 16   C. 24   D. 48

KEY (CORRECT ANSWERS)

1.	B	6.	A	11.	B
2.	B	7.	C	12.	A
3.	A	8.	C	13.	D
4.	D	9.	B	14.	C
5.	A	10.	B	15.	D

SOLUTIONS TO PROBLEMS

1. (26-8)(100-4) = 1728 sq.ft. of usable space

2. 300 1% @ $5.94 = $1782; 150 2% @ $5.88 = $882. $1782 + $882 = $2664

3. (3' 3')(3' 9")(2' 6") = (12)(4)(4) = 192 boxes per carton Then, 1728 192 = 9 cartons

4. (5 1/4')(2 1/3') = 12 1/4 sq.ft. = 12 sq.ft.

5. One man could load 10 trucks in 5 hrs. Thus, 10 men would need 5/10 = 1/2 hr. to load these 10 trucks.

6. 56,000 ÷ 10' = 5600 sq.ft. Selection A which is 70'x80' would yield 5600 sq.ft.

7. (100)(8) = 800 cu.ft., and 800 2 = 400

8. (200')(200') = 40,000 sq.ft. Then, (4000)(2000) 40,000 = 200 lbs. per sq.ft.

9. (1')(1')(3') = 3 cu.ft. = 3/27 = 1/9 cu.yd.

10. $36.00 60 = $.60 per box

11. (100)(2')(1')(1/2') = 100 cu.ft.

12. 30 tons requires (2) (30) = 60 man-hours. Then, 60 10 = 6 men.

13. (100)(20')(22 1/2) = 45,000 lbs.

14. ($1.00)(9')(12')(4) = $432 = $430

15. Each side of board = (2')(12') = 24 sq.ft. Total area = (2) (24) = 48 sq.ft.

EXAMINATION SECTION
TEST 1

DIRECTIONS: Each question or incomplete statement is followed by several suggested answers or completions. Select the one that BEST answers the question or completes the statement. *PRINT THE LETTER OF THE CORRECT ANSWER IN THE SPACE AT THE RIGHT.*

1. Suppose that you are requested to transmit to the stenographers in your bureau an order curtailing certain privileges that they have been enjoying. You anticipate that your staff may resent curtailment of such privileges. Of the following, the BEST action for you to take is to

    A. impress upon your staff that an order is an order and must be obeyed
    B. attempt to explain to your staff the probable reasons for curtailing their privileges
    C. excuse the curtailment of privileges by saying that the welfare of the staff was evidently not considered
    D. warn your staff that violation of an order may be considered sufficient cause for immediate dismissal

1.____

2. The supervisor should set a good example.
Of the following, the CHIEF implication of the above statement is that the supervisor should

    A. behave as he expects his workers to behave
    B. know as much about the work as his workers do
    C. keep his workers informed of what he is doing
    D. keep ahead of his workers

2.____

3. Of the following, the LEAST desirable procedure for the competent supervisor to follow is to

    A. organize his work before taking responsibility for helping others with theirs
    B. avoid schedules and routines when he is busy
    C. be flexible in planning and carrying out his responsibilities
    D. secure the support of his staff in organizing the total job of the unit

3.____

4. Evaluation helps the worker by increasing his security.
Of the following, the BEST justification for this statement is that

    A. security and growth depend upon knowledge by the worker of the agency's evaluation
    B. knowledge of his evaluation by agency and supervisor will stimulate the worker to better performance
    C. evaluation enables the supervisor and worker to determine the reasons for the worker's strengths and weaknesses
    D. the supervisor and worker together can usually recognize and deal with any worker's insecurity

4.____

5. A supervisor may encourage his subordinates to make suggestions by

    A. keeping a record of the number of suggestions an employee makes
    B. providing a suggestion box

5.____

C. outlining a list of possible suggestions
D. giving credit to a subordinate whose suggestion has been accepted and used

6. If you were required to give service ratings to employees under your supervision, you should consider as MOST important during the current period the

   A. personal characteristics and salary and grade of an employee
   B. length of service and the volume of work performed
   C. previous service rating given him
   D. personal characteristics and the quality of work of an employee

7. A supervisor must consider many factors in evaluating a worker whom he has supervised for a considerable time. In evaluating the capacity of such a worker to use independent judgment, the one of the following to which the supervisor should generally give MOST consideration is the worker's

   A. capacity to establish good relationships with people (clients and colleagues)
   B. educational background
   C. emotional stability
   D. the quality and judgment shown by the investigator in previous work situations known to the supervisor

8. Experts in the field of personnel relations feel that it is generally a bad practice for subordinate employees to become aware of pending or contemplated changes in policy or organizational set-up via the "grapevine" CHIEFLY because

   A. evidence that one or more responsible officials have proved untrustworthy will undermine confidence in the agency
   B. the information disseminated by this method is seldom entirely accurate and generally spreads needless unrest among the subordinate staff
   C. the subordinate staff may conclude that the administration feels the staff cannot be trusted with the true information
   D. the subordinate staff may conclude that the administration lacks the courage to make an unpopular announcement through official channels

9. Assume that a supervisor praises his subordinates for satisfactory aspects of their work only when he is about to criticize them for unsatisfactory aspects of their work. Such a practice is UNDESIRABLE primarily because

   A. his subordinates may expect to be praised for their work even if it is unsatisfactory
   B. praising his subordinates for some aspects of their work while criticizing other aspects will weaken the effects of the criticisms
   C. his subordinates would be more receptive to criticism if it were followed by praise
   D. his subordinates may come to disregard praise and wait for criticism to be given

10. The one of the following which would be the BEST reason for an agency to eliminate a procedure for obtaining and recording certain information is that

    A. it is no longer legally required to obtain the information
    B. there is an advantage in obtaining the information
    C. the information could be compiled on the basis of other information available
    D. the information obtained is sometimes incorrect

11. In determining the type and number of records to be kept in an agency, it is important to recognize that records are of value PRIMARILY as

   A. raw material to be used in statistical analysis
   B. sources of information about the agency's activities
   C. by-products of the activities carried on by the agency
   D. data for evaluating the effectiveness of the agency

12. Assume that you are a supervisor. One of the workers under your supervision is careless about the routine aspects of his work.
Of the following, the action MOST likely to develop in this worker a better attitude toward job routines is to demonstrate that

   A. it is just as easy to do his job the right way
   B. organization of his job will leave more time for field work
   C. the routine part of the job is essential to performing a good piece of work
   D. job routines are a responsibility of the worker

13. A supervisor can MOST effectively secure necessary improvement in a worker's office work by

   A. encouraging the worker to keep abreast of his work
   B. relating the routine part of his job to the total job to be done
   C. helping the worker to establish a good system for covering his office work and holding him to it
   D. informing the worker that he will be required to organize his work more efficiently

14. A supervisor should offer criticism in such a manner that the criticism is helpful and not overwhelming.
Of the following, the LEAST valid inference that can be drawn on the basis of the above statement is that a supervisor should

   A. demonstrate that the criticism is partial and not total
   B. give criticism in such a way that it does not undermine the worker's self-confidence
   C. keep his relationships with the worker objective
   D. keep criticism directed towards general work performance

15. The one of the following areas in which a worker may LEAST reasonably expect direct assistance from the supervisor is in

   A. building up rapport with all clients
   B. gaining insight into the unmet needs of clients
   C. developing an understanding of community resources
   D. interpreting agency policies and procedures

16. You are informed that a worker under your supervision has submitted a letter complaining of unfair service rating. Of the following, the MOST valid assumption for you to make concerning this worker is that he should be

   A. more adequately supervised in the future
   B. called in for a supervisory conference
   C. given a transfer to some other unit where he may be more happy
   D. given no more consideration than any other inefficient worker

17. Assume that you are a supervisor. You find that a somewhat bewildered worker, newly appointed to the department, hesitates to ask questions for fear of showing his ignorance and jeopardizing his position.
Of the following, the BEST procedure for you to follow is to

   A. try to discover the reason for his evident fear of authority
   B. tell him that when he is in doubt about a procedure or a policy he should consult his fellow workers
   C. develop with the worker a plan for more frequent supervisory conferences
   D. explain why each staff member is eager to give him available information that will help him do a good job

18. In order to teach an employee to develop an objective approach, the BEST action for the supervisor to take is to help the worker to

   A. develop a sincere interest in his job
   B. understand the varied responsibilities that are an integral part of his job
   C. differentiate clearly between himself as a friend and as an employee
   D. find satisfaction in his work

19. Of the following, the MOST effective method of helping a newly appointed employee adjust to his new job is to

   A. assure him that with experience his uncertain attitudes will be replaced by a professional approach
   B. help him, by accepting him as he is, to have confidence in his ability to handle the job
   C. help him to be on guard against the development of punitive attitudes
   D. help him to recognize the mutability of the agency's policies and procedures

20. Suppose that, as a supervisor, you have scheduled an individual conference with an experienced employee under your supervision.
Of the following, the BEST plan of action for this conference is to

   A. discuss the work that the employee is most interested in
   B. plan with the employee to cover any problems that are difficult for him
   C. advise the employee that the conference is his to do with as he sees fit
   D. spot check the employee's work in advance and select those areas for discussion in which the employee has done poor work

21. Of the following, the CHIEF function of a supervisor should be to

   A. assist in the planning of new policies and the evaluation of existing ones
   B. promote congenial relationships among members of the staff
   C. achieve optimum functioning of each unit and each worker
   D. promote the smooth functioning of job routines

22. The competent supervisor must realize the importance of planning.
Of the following, the aspect of planning which is LEAST appropriately considered a responsibility of the supervisor is

   A. long-range planning for the proper functioning of his unit
   B. planning to take care of peak and slack periods
   C. planning to cover agency policies in group conferences

D. long-range planning to develop community resources

23. The one of the following objectives which should be of LEAST concern to the supervisor in the performance of his duties is to   23._____

    A. help the worker to make friends with all of his fellow employees
    B. be impartial and fair to all members of the staff
    C. stimulate the worker's growth on the job
    D. meet the needs of the individual employee

24. The one of the following which is LEAST properly considered a direct responsibility of the supervisor is   24._____

    A. liaison between the staff and the administrator
    B. interpreting administrative orders and procedures to the employee
    C. training new employees
    D. maintaining staff morale at a high level

25. If an employee shows excessive submission which indicates a need for dependence on the supervisor in handling an assignment, it would be MOST advisable for the supervisor to   25._____

    A. indicate firmly that the employee-supervisor relationship does not call for submission
    B. define areas of responsibility of employee and of superior
    C. recognize the employee's need to be sustained and supported and help him by making decisions for him
    D. encourage the employee to do his best to overcome his handicap

KEY (CORRECT ANSWERS)

1.	B		11.	B
2.	A		12.	D
3.	B		13.	B
4.	C		14.	D
5.	D		15.	A
6.	D		16.	B
7.	D		17.	C
8.	B		18.	C
9.	D		19.	B
10.	C		20.	B

21. C
22. D
23. A
24. A
25. B

TEST 2

DIRECTIONS: Each question or incomplete statement is followed by several suggested answers or completions. Select the one that BEST answers the question or completes the statement. *PRINT THE LETTER OF THE CORRECT ANSWER IN THE SPACE AT THE RIGHT.*

1. Assume that, as a supervisor, you are conducting a group conference. Of the following, the BEST procedure for you to follow in order to stimulate group discussion is to

   A. permit the active participation of all members
   B. direct the discussion to an acceptable conclusion
   C. resolve conflicts of opinion among members of the group
   D. present a question for discussion on which the group members have some knowledge or experience

2. Suppose that, as a new supervisor, you wish to inform the staff under your supervision of your methods of operation. Of the following, the BEST procedure for you to follow is to

   A. advise the staff that they will learn gradually from experience
   B. inform each employee in an individual conference
   C. call a group conference for this purpose
   D. distribute a written memorandum among all members of the staff

3. The MOST constructive and effective method of correcting an employee who has made a mistake is, in general, to

   A. explain that his evaluation is related to his errors
   B. point out immediately where he erred and tell him how it should have been done
   C. show him how to readjust his methods so as to avoid similar errors in the future
   D. try to discover by an indirect method why the error was made

4. The MOST effective method for the supervisor to follow in order to obtain the cooperation of an employee under his supervision is, wherever possible, to

   A. maintain a careful record of performance in order to keep the employee on his toes
   B. give the employee recognition in order to promote greater effort and give him more satisfaction in his work
   C. try to gain the employee's cooperation for the good of the service
   D. advise the employee that his advancement on the job depends on his cooperation

5. Of the following, the MOST appropriate initial course for an employee to take when he is unable to clarify a policy with his supervisor is to

   A. bring up the problem at the next group conference
   B. discuss the policy immediately with his fellow employees
   C. accept the supervisor's interpretation as final
   D. determine what responsibility he has for putting the policy into effect

6. Good administration allows for different treatment of different workers. Of the following, the CHIEF implication of this quotation is that

108

A. it would be unfair for the supervisor not to treat all staff members alike
B. fear of favoritism tends to undermine staff morale
C. best results are obtained by individualization within the limits of fair treatment
D. difficult problems call for a different kind of approach

7. The MOST effective and appropriate method of building efficiency and morale in a group of employees is, in general,

   A. by stressing the economic motive
   B. through use of the authority inherent in the position
   C. by a friendly approach to all
   D. by a discipline that is fair but strict

8. Of the following, the LEAST valid basis for the assignment of work to an employee is the

   A. kind of service to be rendered
   B. experience and training of the employee
   C. health and capacity of the employee
   D. racial composition of the community where the office is located

9. The CHIEF justification for staff education, consisting of in-service training, lies in its contribution to

   A. improvement in the quality of work performed
   B. recruitment of a better type of employee
   C. employee morale accruing from a feeling of growth on the job
   D. the satisfaction that the employee gets on his job

10. Suppose that you are a supervisor. An employee no longer with your department requests you, as his former supervisor, to write a letter recommending him for a position with a private organization.
    Of the following, the BEST procedure for you to follow is to include in the letter only information that

    A. will help the applicant get the job
    B. is clear, factual, and substantiated
    C. is known to you personally
    D. can readily be corroborated by personal interview

11. Of the following, the MOST important item on which to base the efficiency evaluation of an employee under your supervision is

    A. the nature of the relationship that he has built up with his fellow employees
    B. how he gets along with his supervisors
    C. his personal habits and skills
    D. the effectiveness of his control over his work

12. According to generally accepted personnel practice, the MOST effective method of building morale in a new employee is to

    A. exercise caution in praising the employee, lest he become overconfident
    B. give sincere and frank commendation whenever possible, in order to stimulate interest and effort

C. praise the employee highly even for mediocre performance so that he will be stimulated to do better
D. warn the employee frequently that he cannot hope to succeed unless he puts forth his best effort

13. Errors made by newly appointed employees often follow a predictable pattern. The one of the following errors likely to have LEAST serious consequences is the tendency of a new employee to

    A. discuss problems that are outside his province with the client
    B. persuade the client to accept the worker's solution of a problem
    C. be too strict in carrying out departmental policy and procedure
    D. depend upon the use of authority due to his inexperience and lack of skill in working with people

14. The MOST effective way for a supervisor to break down a worker's defensive stand against supervisory guidance is to

    A. come to an understanding with him on the mutual responsibilities involved in the job of the employee and supervisor
    B. tell him he must feel free to express his opinions and to discuss basic problems
    C. show him how to develop toward greater objectivity, sensitivity, and understanding
    D. advise him that it is necessary to carry out agency policy and procedures in order to do a good job

15. Of the following, the LEAST essential function of the supervisor who is conducting a group conference should be to

    A. keep attention focused on the purpose of the conference
    B. encourage discussion of controversial points
    C. make certain that all possible viewpoints are discussed
    D. be thoroughly prepared in advance

16. When conducting a group conference, the supervisor should be LEAST concerned with

    A. providing an opportunity for the free interchange of ideas
    B. imparting knowledge and understanding of case work
    C. leading the discussion toward a planned goal
    D. pointing out where individual workers have erred in work practice

17. If the participants in a group conference are unable to agree on the proper application of a concept to the work of a department, the MOST suitable temporary procedure for the supervisor to follow is to

    A. suggest that each member think the subject through before the next meeting
    B. tell the group to examine their differences for possible conflicts with present policies
    C. suggest that practices can be changed because of new conditions
    D. state the acceptable practice in the agency and whether deviations from such practice can be permitted

18. If an employee is to participate constructively in any group discussion, it is MOST important that he have

    A. advance notice of the agenda for the meeting
    B. long experience in the department
    C. knowledge and experience in the particular work
    D. the ability to assume a leadership role

19. Of the following, the MOST important principle for the supervisor to follow when conducting a group discussion is that he should

    A. move the discussion toward acceptance by the group of a particular point of view
    B. express his ideas clearly and succinctly
    C. lead the group to accept the authority inherent in his position
    D. contribute to the discussion from his knowledge and experience

20. The one of the following which is considered LEAST important as a purpose of the group conference is to

    A. provide for a free exchange of ideas among the members of the group
    B. evaluate work methods and procedures in order to protect the members from individual criticism
    C. provide an opportunity to interpret procedures and work practices
    D. pool the experience of the group members for the benefit of all

21. In order for the evaluation conference to stimulate MOST effectively the employee's professional growth on the job, it should

    A. start him thinking, about his present status with the department
    B. show him the necessity for taking stock of his total performance
    C. give him a sense of direction in relation to his future development
    D. give him a better perspective on the work in his department

22. The development of good public relations in the area for which the supervisor is responsible should be considered by the supervisor as

    A. not his responsibility as he is primarily responsible for his employees' services
    B. dependent upon him as he is in the best position to interpret the department to the community
    C. not important to the adequate functioning of the department
    D. a part of his method of carrying out his job responsibility, as what his employees do affect the community

23. Of the following, the MOST valuable and desirable trait in a supervisor is a(n)

    A. ability to get the best work out of his men
    B. ability to inspire his men with the desire to "get ahead in the world"
    C. persuasive manner of speech
    D. tall and commanding appearance

24. The supervisor who is MOST suitable for the general practical needs of a department is the one who gets 24.___

    A. a great deal of satisfactory work done although usually handicapped by constant bickering among fellow employees
    B. a great deal of satisfactory work done because of his ability to do a large amount of it himself
    C. less work done than the other supervisors but has unusually high quality work production standards
    D. more than an average amount of satisfactory work done because of the cooperative way in which the employees work for him

25. A supervisor has been transferred to a new section. 25.___
The BEST way for him to get cooperation from his employees would be to

    A. ask the (general manager)(chief) to give him strong support
    B. explain his policy firmly so that the employees cannot blame him for any mistakes made
    C. note the troublemakers and have them transferred out
    D. show his men that he not only is interested in getting work done but also has their welfare in mind

KEY (CORRECT ANSWERS)

1.	D	11.	D
2.	C	12.	B
3.	C	13.	C
4.	B	14.	A
5.	D	15.	B
6.	C	16.	D
7.	D	17.	D
8.	D	18.	A
9.	A	19.	D
10.	B	20.	B

21. C
22. D
23. A
24. D
25. D

TEST 3

DIRECTIONS: Each question or incomplete statement is followed by several suggested answers or completions. Select the one that BEST answers the question or completes the statement. *PRINT THE LETTER OF THE CORRECT ANSWER IN THE SPACE AT THE RIGHT.*

1. Jones and Smith, who work together, do slightly more than an average amount of work for two men together. But you find that Jones does most of the work while Smith does less than he should.
   To correct this situation, the BEST thing for you as supervisor to do would be to

   A. assign work to Smith for which he must be personally responsible
   B. make a complaint to the bureau chief about Smith but praise Jones
   C. point out to Jones that he does most of the work and that he should urge Smith to do more
   D. require Smith to do more whenever the work of both men together falls below the expected average

   1.____

2. You have given a new employee detailed instructions on how he should do a job. When you return a little later, you find that the employee was afraid to start the job because he did not completely understand your instructions.
   In this situation, it would be BEST for you to

   A. assign the man to a job where less intelligence is needed
   B. explain again, illustrating if possible how the job is to be done
   C. explain again and recommend him for dropping at the end of probation if he does not understand
   D. make the man explain why he did not at least start the job

   2.____

3. An employee does very good work but has trouble getting to work on time.
   To get him to come on time, the supervisor should

   A. bring him up on charges to stop the lateness once and for all
   B. have him report to the general manager every time he is late
   C. talk over the problem with him to find its cause and possible solution
   D. threaten to transfer him if he cannot get to work early

   3.____

4. As supervisor, you observe that an employee keeps making mistakes.
   Of the following, the BEST thing for you to do would be to

   A. make no mention of these mistakes as they gradually disappear with experience
   B. point the mistakes out to the employee in front of the other employees so all may learn from them
   C. talk to the employee privately about these mistakes and show her how to avoid them
   D. try to transfer this employee out in exchange for an employee who can do the work

   4.____

5. Proper action by the supervisor could MOST probably prevent work delays in his section caused by

   A. a large number of employees quitting their jobs in the department
   B. the daily assignments of the employees not being properly planned

   5.____

113

C. the inexperience of new employees transferred into his section
D. unexpected delays in processing

6. If, after careful thought, you have definitely decided that one of your employees should be disciplined, it is MOST important for you to realize that

    A. discipline is the best tool for leading workers
    B. discipline should be severe in order to get the best results
    C. the discipline should be delayed so that its full force can be felt
    D. the employee should know why she is being disciplined

7. A knowledge of the experience and abilities of the men working under him is MOST useful to a supervisor in

    A. deciding what type of discipline to exercise when necessary
    B. finding the cause of minor errors in the assignments
    C. making proper work assignments
    D. making vacation schedules

8. A supervisor will be able to train his employees better if he is familiar with basic principles of learning.
Which one of the following statements about the learning process is MOST correct?

    A. An employee who learns one job quickly will learn any other job quickly.
    B. Emphasizing correct things done by the employee usually gives him an incentive to improve.
    C. Great importance placed on an employee's mistakes is the best way to help him to get rid of them.
    D. It is very hard to teach new methods to middle-aged or older employees.

9. Several experienced employees have resigned. You have decided to arrange for permanent transfers of other experienced employees in your section to fill their jobs, leaving only jobs that new inexperienced employees can fill easily.
For you, the supervisor, to talk this over with the employees who will be affected by the move would be

    A. *bad;* it would show weakness and wavering by you
    B. *bad;* transfers should be made on the basis of efficiency
    C. *good;* it will help you get better cooperation from the employees involved
    D. *good;* transfers should be made on the basis of seniority

10. An employee under your supervision does much less work than he is capable of.
What should be your FIRST step in an effort to improve his performance?

    A. Discovering why he is not working up to his full capacity
    B. Going over his mistakes and shortcomings with him to reduce them
    C. Pointing out to him that the quality of his work is below standard
    D. Showing him that the other men produce much more than he does

11. The FIRST thing a supervisor does when he assigns an employee to a new job is to find out what the employee already knows about the job.
This practice is

A. *good;* mainly because the employees may know more than the supervisor about the job
B. *good;* mainly because this information will help the supervisor in instructing the employee
C. *poor;* mainly because since it is a new job, the employee cannot be expected to know anything
D. *poor;* mainly because the supervisor should first find out how the employee will feel toward the job

12. Your superior has assigned to you a task which, in your opinion, should not be performed at this stage of the operation.
In this situation, it would be BEST for you to

   A. carry out the assignment since your superior is responsible
   B. refuse to carry out the assignment
   C. talk it over with the employees under you to see if they think as you do
   D. talk the matter over with your superior right away

12.____

13. It is important for a supervisor to take prompt action upon requests from subordinates MAINLY because

   A. delays in making decisions mean that they must then be made on the basis of facts which can no longer be up-to-date
   B. favorable action on such requests is more likely to result when a decision is made quickly
   C. it is an indication that the supervisor has his work well-organized
   D. promptness in such matters helps maintain good employee morale

13.____

14. As a supervisor, you realize that your superior, when under pressure, has a habit of giving you oral orders which are not always clear and also lack sufficient detail. The BEST procedure for you to follow in such situations would be to

   A. obtain clarification by requesting needed details at the time you receive such orders
   B. consider past orders of a similar nature to determine the probable intent of your superior
   C. frequently consult your superior during the course of the job in order to secure the required details to complete the job
   D. request your superior to put all his orders to you in writing

14.____

15. Some supervisors have their subordinates meet with them in group discussion of troublesome problems.
The MAIN advantage of such group discussions as a supervisory tool is that they can be directed toward the

   A. appraisal of the personalities involved
   B. development of new policies and regulations
   C. circulation of new material and information
   D. pooling of experience in the solution of common problems

15.____

16. The PRINCIPAL disadvantage of using form letters to reply to written complaints made by the public is that such form letters

16.____

A. tend to make any investigation of the original complaint rather superficial
B. are limited by their design to handle only a few possible situations that could give rise to complaints
C. lack the desirable element of the personal touch for the recipient
D. tend to lose their effectiveness by quickly becoming obsolete

17. With respect to standard employee grievance procedure, it would be MOST correct to state that

   A. the Commissioner of Labor is the highest ranking official, excepting the judge, who can be involved in a particular grievance
   B. the person with the grievance has the right to be represented by virtually anyone he chooses
   C. the one having the grievance (the grievant) can be represented by the majority organization only if he is a member thereof
   D. time limits are not set concerning adjudication in order to insure the fullest consideration of the particular grievance

18. In order for a supervisor to employ the system of democratic leadership in his supervision, it would generally be BEST for him to

   A. allow his subordinates to assist in deciding on methods of work performance and job assignments but only in those areas where decisions have not been made on higher administrative levels
   B. allow his subordinates to decide how to do the required work, interposing his authority when work is not completed on schedule or is improperly completed
   C. attempt to make assignments of work to individuals only of the type which they enjoy doing
   D. maintain control over the job assignments and work production but allow the subordinates to select methods of work and internal conditions of work at democratically conducted staff conferences

19. In an office in which supervision has been considered quite effective, it has become necessary to press for above-normal production for a limited period to achieve a required goal.
The one of the following which is a LEAST likely result of this pressure is that

   A. there will be more "gripings" by employees
   B. some workers will do both more and better work than has been normal for them
   C. there will be an enhanced feeling of group unity
   D. there will be increased absenteeism

20. It is the practice of some supervisors, when they believe that it would be desirable for a subordinate to take a particular action in a case, to inform the subordinate of this in the form of a suggestion rather than in the form of a direct order. In general, this method of getting a subordinate to take the desired action is

   A. *inadvisable;* it may create in the mind of the subordinate the impression that the supervisor is uncertain about the efficacy of his plan and is trying to avoid whatever responsibility he may have in resolving the case
   B. *advisable;* it provides the subordinate with the maximum opportunity to use his own judgment in handling the case

C. *inadvisable;* it provides the subordinate with no clear-cut direction and, therefore, is likely to leave him with a feeling of uncertainty and frustration
D. *advisable;* it presents the supervisor's view in a manner which will be most likely to evoke the subordinate's cooperation

21. At a group training conference conducted by a supervisor, one of the employees asks a question which is only partially related to the subject under discussion. He believes that the question was asked to embarrass him since he recently reprimanded the employees for inattention to his work. Under these circumstances, it would generally be BEST for the assistant supervisor to

    A. pointedly ignore the question and the questioner and go on to other matters
    B. request the questioner to remain after the group session, at which time the question and the questioner's attitude will be considered
    C. state that he does not know the answer and ask for a volunteer to give a brief answer, brief because the question is only partially relevant
    D. tell the questioner that the question is not pertinent, show wherein it is not pertinent, and state that the time of the group should not be wasted on it

22. The one of the following circumstances when it would generally be MOST proper for a supervisor to do a job himself rather than to train a subordinate to do the job is when it is

    A. a job which the supervisor enjoys doing and does well
    B. not a very time-consuming job but an important one
    C. difficult to train another to do the job yet is not difficult for the supervisor to do
    D. unlikely that this or any similar job will have to be done again at any future time

23. Effective training of subordinates requires that the supervisor understand certain facts about learning and forgetting processes.
    Among these is the fact that people generally

    A. both learn and forget at a relatively constant rate and this rate is dependent upon their general intellectual capacity
    B. forget what they learned at a much greater rate during the first day than during subsequent periods
    C. learn at a relatively constant rate except for periods of assimilation when the quantity of retained learning decreases while information is becoming firmly fixed in the mind
    D. learn very slowly at first when introduced to a new topic, after which there is a great increase in the rate of learning

24. It has been suggested that a subordinate who likes his supervisor will tend to do better work than one who does not. According to the MOST widely-held current theories of supervision, this suggestion is a

    A. *bad one;* since personal relationships tend to interfere with proper professional relationships
    B. *bad one;* since the strongest motivating factors are fear and uncertainty
    C. *good one;* since liking one's supervisor is a motivating factor for good work performance
    D. *good one;* since liking one's supervisor is the most important factor in employee performance

25. A supervisor is supervising an employee who is very soon to complete his six months' probationary period. The supervisor finds him to be slow, to make many errors, to do work poorly, to be antagonistic toward the supervisor, and to be disliked by most of his co-workers. The supervisor is aware that he is the sole support of his wife and two children. He has never been late or absent during his service with the department. If he is terminated, there will be a considerable delay before a replacement for him arrives.
It would generally be BEST for the supervisor to recommend that this employee be

    A. transferred to work with another supervisor and other staff members with whom he may get along better
    B. retained but be very closely supervised until his work shows marked improvement
    C. retained since his services are needed with the expectation that he be terminated at some later date when a replacement is readily available
    D. terminated

KEY (CORRECT ANSWERS)

1.	A		11.	B
2.	B		12.	D
3.	C		13.	D
4.	C		14.	A
5.	B		15.	D
6.	D		16.	C
7.	C		17.	B
8.	B		18.	A
9.	C		19.	D
10.	A		20.	D

21.	C
22.	D
23.	B
24.	C
25.	D

PHILOSOPHY, PRINCIPLES, PRACTICES AND TECHNICS
OF
SUPERVISION, ADMINISTRATION, MANAGEMENT AND ORGANIZATION

TABLE OF CONTENTS

		Page
I.	MEANING OF SUPERVISION	1
II.	THE OLD AND THE NEW SUPERVISION	1
III.	THE EIGHT (8) BASIC PRINCIPLES OF THE NEW SUPERVISION	1
	1. Principle of Responsibility	1
	2. Principle of Authority	2
	3. Principle of Self-Growth	2
	4. Principle of Individual Worth	2
	5. Principle of Creative Leadership	2
	6. Principle of Success and Failure	2
	7. Principle of Science	3
	8. Principle of Cooperation	3
IV.	WHAT IS ADMINISTRATION?	3
	1. Practices commonly classed as "Supervisory"	3
	2. Practices commonly classed as "Administrative"	3
	3. Practices classified as both "Supervisory" and "Administrative"	4
V.	RESPONSIBILITIES OF THE SUPERVISOR	4
VI.	COMPETENCIES OF THE SUPERVISOR	4
VII.	THE PROFESSIONAL SUPERVISOR—EMPLOYEE RELATIONSHIP	4
VIII.	MINI-TEXT IN SUPERVISION, ADMINISTRATION, MANAGEMENT AND ORGANIZATION	5
	A. Brief Highlights	5
	1. Levels of Management	5
	2. What the Supervisor Must Learn	6
	3. A Definition of Supervision	6
	4. Elements of the Team Concept	6
	5. Principles of Organization	6
	6. The Four Important Parts of Every Job	6
	7. Principles of Delegation	6
	8. Principles of Effective Communications	7
	9. Principles of Work Improvement	7

TABLE OF CONTENTS (CONTINUED)

10. Areas of Job Improvement	7
11. Seven Key Points in Making Improvements	7
12. Corrective Techniques for Job Improvement	7
13. A Planning Checklist	8
14. Five Characteristics of Good Directions	8
15. Types of Directions	8
16. Controls	8
17. Orienting the New Employee	8
18. Checklist for Orienting New Employees	8
19. Principles of Learning	9
20. Causes of Poor Performance	9
21. Four Major Steps in On-The-Job Instructions	9
22. Employees Want Five Things	9
23. Some Don'ts in Regard to Praise	9
24. How to Gain Your Workers' Confidence	9
25. Sources of Employee Problems	9
26. The Supervisor's Key to Discipline	10
27. Five Important Processes of Management	10
28. When the Supervisor Fails to Plan	10
29. Fourteen General Principles of Management	10
30. Change	10
B. Brief Topical Summaries	11
I. Who/What is the Supervisor?	11
II. The Sociology of Work	11
III. Principles and Practices of Supervision	12
IV. Dynamic Leadership	12
V. Processes for Solving Problems	12
VI. Training for Results	13
VII. Health, Safety and Accident Prevention	13
VIII. Equal Employment Opportunity	13
IX. Improving Communications	14
X. Self-Development	14
XI. Teaching and Training	14
A. The Teaching Process	14
1. Preparation	14
2. Presentation	15
3. Summary	15
4. Application	15
5. Evaluation	15
B. Teaching Methods	15
1. Lecture	15
2. Discussion	15
3. Demonstration	16
4. Performance	16
5. Which Method to Use	16

PHILOSOPHY, PRINCIPLES, PRACTICES, AND TECHNICS
OF
SUPERVISION, ADMINISTRATION, MANAGEMENT AND ORGANIZATION

I. MEANING OF SUPERVISION

The extension of the democratic philosophy has been accompanied by an extension in the scope of supervision. Modern leaders and supervisors no longer think of supervision in the narrow sense of being confined chiefly to visiting employees, supplying materials, or rating the staff. They regard supervision as being intimately related to all the concerned agencies of society, they speak of the supervisor's function in terms of "growth", rather than the "improvement," of employees.

This modern concept of supervision may be defined as follows:

Supervision is leadership and the development of leadership within groups which are cooperatively engaged in inspection, research, training, guidance and evaluation.

II. THE OLD AND THE NEW SUPERVISION

TRADITIONAL
1. Inspection
2. Focused on the employee
3. Visitation
4. Random and haphazard
5. Imposed and authoritarian
6. One person usually

MODERN
1. Study and analysis
2. Focused on aims, materials, methods, supervisors, employees, environment
3. Demonstrations, intervisitation, workshops, directed reading, bulletins, etc.
4. Definitely organized and planned (scientific)
5. Cooperative and democratic
6. Many persons involved (creative)

III THE EIGHT (8) BASIC PRINCIPLES OF THE NEW SUPERVISION

1. *PRINCIPLE OF RESPONSIBILITY*
Authority to act and responsibility for acting must be joined.
   a. If you give responsibility, give authority.
   b. Define employee duties clearly.
   c. Protect employees from criticism by others.
   d. Recognize the rights as well as obligations of employees.
   e. Achieve the aims of a democratic society insofar as it is possible within the area of your work.
   f. Establish a situation favorable to training and learning.
   g. Accept ultimate responsibility for everything done in your section, unit, office, division, department.
   h. Good administration and good supervision are inseparable.

2. PRINCIPLE OF AUTHORITY

The success of the supervisor is measured by the extent to which the power of authority is not used.
- a. Exercise simplicity and informality in supervision.
- b. Use the simplest machinery of supervision.
- c. If it is good for the organization as a whole, it is probably justified.
- d. Seldom be arbitrary or authoritative.
- e. Do not base your work on the power of position or of personality.
- f. Permit and encourage the free expression of opinions.

3. PRINCIPLE OF SELF-GROWTH

The success of the supervisor is measured by the extent to which, and the speed with which, he is no longer needed.
- a. Base criticism on principles, not on specifics.
- b. Point out higher activities to employees.
- c. Train for self-thinking by employees, to meet new situations.
- d. Stimulate initiative, self-reliance and individual responsibility.
- e. Concentrate on stimulating the growth of employees rather than on removing defects.

4. PRINCIPLE OF INDIVIDUAL WORTH

Respect for the individual is a paramount consideration in supervision.
- a. Be human and sympathetic in dealing with employees.
- b. Don't nag about things to be done.
- c. Recognize the individual differences among employees and seek opportunities to permit best expression of each personality.

5. PRINCIPLE OF CREATIVE LEADERSHIP

The best supervision is that which is not apparent to the employee.
- a. Stimulate, don't drive employees to creative action.
- b. Emphasize doing good things.
- c. Encourage employees to do what they do best.
- d. Do not be too greatly concerned with details of subject or method.
- e. Do not be concerned exclusively with immediate problems and activities.
- f. Reveal higher activities and make them both desired and maximally possible.
- g. Determine procedures in the light of each situation but see that these are derived from a sound basic philosophy.
- h. Aid, inspire and lead so as to liberate the creative spirit latent in all good employees.

6. PRINCIPLE OF SUCCESS AND FAILURE

There are no unsuccessful employees, only unsuccessful supervisors who have failed to give proper leadership.
- a. Adapt suggestions to the capacities, attitudes, and prejudices of employees.
- b. Be gradual, be progressive, be persistent.
- c. Help the employee find the general principle; have the employee apply his own problem to the general principle.
- d. Give adequate appreciation for good work and honest effort.
- e. Anticipate employee difficulties and help to prevent them.
- f. Encourage employees to do the desirable things they will do anyway.
- g. Judge your supervision by the results it secures.

7. PRINCIPLE OF SCIENCE

Successful supervision is scientific, objective, and experimental. It is based on facts, not on prejudices.
    a. Be cumulative in results.
    b. Never divorce your suggestions from the goals of training.
    c. Don't be impatient of results.
    d. Keep all matters on a professional, not a personal level.
    e. Do not be concerned exclusively with immediate problems and activities.
    f. Use objective means of determining achievement and rating where possible.

8. PRINCIPLE OF COOPERATION

Supervision is a cooperative enterprise between supervisor and employee.
    a. Begin with conditions as they are.
    b. Ask opinions of all involved when formulating policies.
    c. Organization is as good as its weakest link.
    d. Let employees help to determine policies and department programs.
    e. Be approachable and accessible - physically and mentally.
    f. Develop pleasant social relationships.

IV. WHAT IS ADMINISTRATION?

Administration is concerned with providing the environment, the material facilities, and the operational procedures that will promote the maximum growth and development of supervisors and employees. (Organization is an aspect, and a concomitant, of administration.)

There is no sharp line of demarcation between supervision and administration; these functions are intimately interrelated and, often, overlapping. They are complementary activities.

1. PRACTICES COMMONLY CLASSED AS "SUPERVISORY"
    a. Conducting employees conferences
    b. Visiting sections, units, offices, divisions, departments
    c. Arranging for demonstrations
    d. Examining plans
    e. Suggesting professional reading
    f. Interpreting bulletins
    g. Recommending in-service training courses
    h. Encouraging experimentation
    i. Appraising employee morale
    j. Providing for intervisitation

2. PRACTICES COMMONLY CLASSIFIED AS "ADMINISTRATIVE"
    a. Management of the office
    b. Arrangement of schedules for extra duties
    c. Assignment of rooms or areas
    d. Distribution of supplies
    e. Keeping records and reports
    f. Care of audio-visual materials
    g. Keeping inventory records
    h. Checking record cards and books
    i. Programming special activities
    j. Checking on the attendance and punctuality of employees

3. *PRACTICES COMMONLY CLASSIFIED AS BOTH "SUPERVISORY" AND "ADMINISTRATIVE"*
   a. Program construction
   b. Testing or evaluating outcomes
   c. Personnel accounting
   d. Ordering instructional materials

V. RESPONSIBILITIES OF THE SUPERVISOR

A person employed in a supervisory capacity must constantly be able to improve his own efficiency and ability. He represents the employer to the employees and only continuous self-examination can make him a capable supervisor.

Leadership and training are the supervisor's responsibility. An efficient working unit is one in which the employees work with the supervisor. It is his job to bring out the best in his employees. He must always be relaxed, courteous and calm in his association with his employees. Their feelings are important, and a harsh attitude does not develop the most efficient employees.

VI. COMPETENCIES OF THE SUPERVISOR

1. Complete knowledge of the duties and responsibilities of his position.
2. To be able to organize a job, plan ahead and carry through.
3. To have self-confidence and initiative.
4. To be able to handle the unexpected situation and make quick decisions.
5. To be able to properly train subordinates in the positions they are best suited for.
6. To be able to keep good human relations among his subordinates.
7. To be able to keep good human relations between his subordinates and himself and to earn their respect and trust.

VII. THE PROFESSIONAL SUPERVISOR-EMPLOYEE RELATIONSHIP

There are two kinds of efficiency: one kind is only apparent and is produced in organizations through the exercise of mere discipline; this is but a simulation of the second, or true, efficiency which springs from spontaneous cooperation. If you are a manager, no matter how great or small your responsibility, it is your job, in the final analysis, to create and develop this involuntary cooperation among the people whom you supervise. For, no matter how powerful a combination of money, machines, and materials a company may have, this is a dead and sterile thing without a team of willing, thinking and articulate people to guide it.

The following 21 points are presented as indicative of the exemplary basic relationship that should exist between supervisor and employee:

1. Each person wants to be liked and respected by his fellow employee and wants to be treated with consideration and respect by his superior.
2. The most competent employee will make an error. However, in a unit where good relations exist between the supervisor and his employees, tenseness and fear do not exist. Thus, errors are not hidden or covered up and the efficiency of a unit is not impaired.
3. Subordinates resent rules, regulations, or orders that are unreasonable or unexplained.
4. Subordinates are quick to resent unfairness, harshness, injustices and favoritism.
5. An employee will accept responsibility if he knows that he will be complimented for a job well done, and not too harshly chastised for failure; that his supervisor will check the cause of the failure, and, if it was the supervisor's fault, he will assume the blame therefore. If it was the employee's fault, his supervisor will explain the correct method or means of handling the responsibility.

6. An employee wants to receive credit for a suggestion he has made, that is used. If a suggestion cannot be used, the employee is entitled to an explanation. The supervisor should not say "no" and close the subject.
7. Fear and worry slow up a worker's ability. Poor working environment can impair his physical and mental health. A good supervisor avoids forceful methods, threats and arguments to get a job done.
8. A forceful supervisor is able to train his employees individually and as a team, and is able to motivate them in the proper channels.
9. A mature supervisor is able to properly evaluate his subordinates and to keep them happy and satisfied.
10. A sensitive supervisor will never patronize his subordinates.
11. A worthy supervisor will respect his employees' confidences.
12. Definite and clear-cut responsibilities should be assigned to each executive.
13. Responsibility should always be coupled with corresponding authority.
14. No change should be made in the scope or responsibilities of a position without a definite understanding to that effect on the part of all persons concerned.
15. No executive or employee, occupying a single position in the organization, should be subject to definite orders from more than one source.
16. Orders should never be given to subordinates over the head of a responsible executive. Rather than do this, the officer in question should be supplanted.
17. Criticisms of subordinates should, whoever possible, be made privately, and in no case should a subordinate be criticized in the presence of executives or employees of equal or lower rank.
18. No dispute or difference between executives or employees as to authority or responsibilities should be considered too trivial for prompt and careful adjudication.
19. Promotions, wage changes, and disciplinary action should always be approved by the executive immediately superior to the one directly responsible.
20. No executive or employee should ever be required, or expected, to be at the same time an assistant to, and critic of, another.
21. Any executive whose work is subject to regular inspection should, whever practicable, be given the assistance and facilities necessary to enable him to maintain an independent check of the quality of his work.

VIII. MINI-TEXT IN SUPERVISION, ADMINISTRATION, MANAGEMENT, AND ORGANIZATION

A. BRIEF HIGHLIGHTS

Listed concisely and sequentially are major headings and important data in the field for quick recall and review.

1. *LEVELS OF MANAGEMENT*

Any organization of some size has several levels of management. In terms of a ladder the levels are:

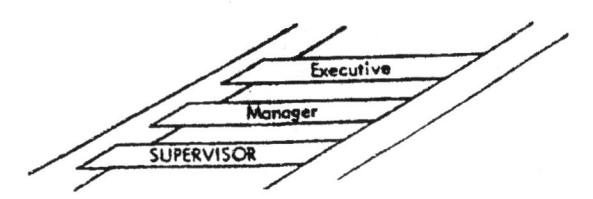

```
        Executive
      Manager
   SUPERVISOR
```

The first level is very important because it is the beginning point of management leadership.

2. WHAT THE SUPERVISOR MUST LEARN
A supervisor must learn to:
- (1) Deal with people and their differences
- (2) Get the job done through people
- (3) Recognize the problems when they exist
- (4) Overcome obstacles to good performance
- (5) Evaluate the performance of people
- (6) Check his own performance in terms of accomplishment

3. A DEFINITION OF SUPERVISOR
The term supervisor means any individual having authority, in the interests of the employer, to hire, transfer, suspend, lay-off, recall, promote, discharge, assign, reward, or discipline other employees or responsibility to direct them, or to adjust their grievances, or effectively to recommend such action, if, in connection with the foregoing, exercise of such authority is not of a merely routine or clerical nature but requires the use of independent judgment.

4. ELEMENTS OF THE TEAM CONCEPT
What is involved in teamwork? The component parts are:
- (1) Members
- (2) A leader
- (3) Goals
- (4) Plans
- (5) Cooperation
- (6) Spirit

5. PRINCIPLES OF ORGANIZATION
- (1) A team member must know what his job is.
- (2) Be sure that the nature and scope of a job are understood.
- (3) Authority and responsibility should be carefully spelled out.
- (4) A supervisor should be permitted to make the maximum number of decisions affecting his employees.
- (5) Employees should report to only one supervisor.
- (6) A supervisor should direct only as many employees as he can handle effectively.
- (7) An organization plan should be flexible.
- (8) Inspection and performance of work should be separate.
- (9) Organizational problems should receive immediate attention.
- (10) Assign work in line with ability and experience.

6. THE FOUR IMPORTANT PARTS OF EVERY JOB
- (1) Inherent in every job is the *accountability* for results.
- (2) A second set of factors in every job is *responsibilities*.
- (3) Along with duties and responsibilities one must have the *authority* to act within certain limits without obtaining permission to proceed.
- (4) No job exists in a vacuum. The supervisor is surrounded by key *relationships*.

7. PRINCIPLES OF DELEGATION
Where work is delegated for the first time, the supervisor should think in terms of these questions:
- (1) Who is best qualified to do this?
- (2) Can an employee improve his abilities by doing this?
- (3) How long should an employee spend on this?
- (4) Are there any special problems for which he will need guidance?
- (5) How broad a delegation can I make?

8. PRINCIPLES OF EFFECTIVE COMMUNICATIONS
    (1) Determine the media
    (2) To whom directed?
    (3) Identification and source authority
    (4) Is communication understood?

9. PRINCIPLES OF WORK IMPROVEMENT
    (1) Most people usually do only the work which is assigned to them
    (2) Workers are likely to fit assigned work into the time available to perform it
    (3) A good workload usually stimulates output
    (4) People usually do their best work when they know that results will be reviewed or inspected
    (5) Employees usually feel that someone else is responsible for conditions of work, workplace layout, job methods, type of tools/equipment, and other such factors
    (6) Employees are usually defensive about their job security
    (7) Employees have natural resistance to change
    (8) Employees can support or destroy a supervisor
    (9) A supervisor usually earns the respect of his people through his personal example of diligence and efficiency

10. AREAS OF JOB IMPROVEMENT
The areas of job improvement are quite numerous, but the most common ones which a supervisor can identify and utilize are:
    (1) Departmental layout
    (2) Flow of work
    (3) Workplace layout
    (4) Utilization of manpower
    (5) Work methods
    (6) Materials handling
    (7) Utilization
    (8) Motion economy

11. SEVEN KEY POINTS IN MAKING IMPROVEMENTS
    (1) Select the job to be improved
    (2) Study how it is being done now
    (3) Question the present method
    (4) Determine actions to be taken
    (5) Chart proposed method
    (6) Get approval and apply
    (7) Solicit worker participation

12. CORRECTIVE TECHNIQUES OF JOB IMPROVEMENT

Specific Problems	General Improvement	Corrective Techniques
(1) Size of workload	(1) Departmental layout	(1) Study with scale model
(2) Inability to meet schedules	(2) Flow of work	(2) Flow chart study
(3) Strain and fatigue	(3) Work plan layout	(3) Motion analysis
(4) Improper use of men and skills	(4) Utilization of manpower	(4) Comparison of units produced to standard allowance
(5) Waste, poor quality, unsafe conditions	(5) Work methods	(5) Methods analysis
(6) Bottleneck conditions that hinder output	(6) Materials handling	(6) Flow chart & equipment study
(7) Poor utilization of equipment and machine	(7) Utilization of equipment	(7) Down time vs. running time
(8) Efficiency and productivity of labor	(8) Motion economy	(8) Motion analysis

13. A PLANNING CHECKLIST

(1) Objectives	(6) Resources	(11) Safety
(2) Controls	(7) Manpower	(12) Money
(3) Delegations	(8) Equipment	(13) Work
(4) Communications	(9) Supplies and materials	(14) Timing of improvements
(5) Resources	(10) Utilization of time	

14. FIVE CHARACTERISTICS OF GOOD DIRECTIONS

In order to get results, directions must be:

(1) Possible of accomplishment
(2) Agreeable with worker interests
(3) Related to mission
(4) Planned and complete
(5) Unmistakably clear

15. TYPES OF DIRECTIONS

(1) Demands or direct orders
(2) Requests
(3) Suggestion or implication
(4) Volunteering

16. CONTROLS

A typical listing of the overall areas in which the supervisor should establish controls might be:

(1) Manpower
(2) Materials
(3) Quality of work
(4) Quantity of work
(5) Time
(6) Space
(7) Money
(8) Methods

17. ORIENTING THE NEW EMPLOYEE

(1) Prepare for him
(2) Welcome the new employee
(3) Orientation for the job
(4) Follow-up

18. CHECKLIST FOR ORIENTING NEW EMPLOYEES

	Yes	No
(1) Do your appreciate the feelings of new employees when they first report for work?	___	___
(2) Are you aware of the fact that the new employee must make a big adjustment to his job?	___	___
(3) Have you given him good reasons for liking the job and the organization?	___	___
(4) Have you prepared for his first day on the job?		
(5) Did you welcome him cordially and make him feel needed?		
(6) Did you establish rapport with him so that he feels free to talk and discuss matters with you?	___	___
(7) Did you explain his job to him and his relationship to you?	___	___
(8) Does he know that his work will be evaluated periodically on a basis that is fair and objective?	___	___
(9) Did you introduce him to his fellow workers in such a way that they are likely to accept him?	___	___
(10) Does he know what employee benefits he will receive?		
(11) Does he understand the importance of being on the job and what to do if he must leave his duty station?	___	___
(12) Has he been impressed with the importance of accident prevention and safe practice?	___	___
(13) Does he generally know his way around the department?	___	___
(14) Is he under the guidance of a sponsor who will teach the right ways of doing things?	___	___
(15) Do you plan to follow-up so that he will continue to adjust successfully to his job?	___	___

19. PRINCIPLES OF LEARNING
(1) Motivation   (2) Demonstration or explanation   (3) Practice

20. CAUSES OF POOR PERFORMANCE
(1) Improper training for job
(2) Wrong tools
(3) Inadequate directions
(4) Lack of supervisory follow-up
(5) Poor communications
(6) Lack of standards of performance
(7) Wrong work habits
(8) Low morale
(9) Other

21. FOUR MAJOR STEPS IN ON-THE-JOB INSTRUCTION
(1) Prepare the worker
(2) Present the operation
(3) Tryout performance
(4) Follow-up

22. EMPLOYEES WANT FIVE THINGS
(1) Security   (2) Opportunity   (3) Recognition   (4) Inclusion   (5) Expression

23. SOME DON'TS IN REGARD TO PRAISE
(1) Don't praise a person for something he hasn't done
(2) Don't praise a person unless you can be sincere
(3) Don't be sparing in praise just because your superior withholds it from you
(4) Don't let too much time elapse between good performance and recognition of it

24. HOW TO GAIN YOUR WORKERS' CONFIDENCE
Methods of developing confidence include such things as:
(1) Knowing the interests, habits, hobbies of employees
(2) Admitting your own inadequacies
(3) Sharing and telling of confidence in others
(4) Supporting people when they are in trouble
(5) Delegating matters that can be well handled
(6) Being frank and straightforward about problems and working conditions
(7) Encouraging others to bring their problems to you
(8) Taking action on problems which impede worker progress

25. SOURCES OF EMPLOYEE PROBLEMS
On-the-job causes might be such things as:
(1) A feeling that favoritism is exercised in assignments
(2) Assignment of overtime
(3) An undue amount of supervision
(4) Changing methods or systems
(5) Stealing of ideas or trade secrets
(6) Lack of interest in job
(7) Threat of reduction in force
(8) Ignorance or lack of communications
(9) Poor equipment
(10) Lack of knowing how supervisor feels toward employee
(11) Shift assignments

Off-the-job problems might have to do with:
(1) Health   (2) Finances   (3) Housing   (4) Family

26. THE SUPERVISOR'S KEY TO DISCIPLINE

There are several key points about discipline which the supervisor should keep in mind:
(1) Job discipline is one of the disciplines of life and is directed by the supervisor.
(2) It is more important to correct an employee fault than to fix blame for it.
(3) Employee performance is affected by problems both on the job and off.
(4) Sudden or abrupt changes in behavior can be indications of important employee problems.
(5) Problems should be dealt with as soon as possible after they are identified.
(6) The attitude of the supervisor may have more to do with solving problems than the techniques of problem solving.
(7) Correction of employee behavior should be resorted to only after the supervisor is sure that training or counseling will not be helpful.
(8) Be sure to document your disciplinary actions.
(9) Make sure that you are disciplining on the basis of facts rather than personal feelings.
(10) Take each disciplinary step in order, being careful not to make snap judgments, or decisions based on impatience.

27. FIVE IMPORTANT PROCESSES OF MANAGEMENT

(1) Planning   (2) Organizing   (3) Scheduling
(4) Controlling   (5) Motivating

28. WHEN THE SUPERVISOR FAILS TO PLAN

(1) Supervisor creates impression of not knowing his job
(2) May lead to excessive overtime
(3) Job runs itself -- supervisor lacks control
(4) Deadlines and appointments missed
(5) Parts of the work go undone
(6) Work interrupted by emergencies
(7) Sets a bad example
(8) Uneven workload creates peaks and valleys
(9) Too much time on minor details at expense of more important tasks

29. FOURTEEN GENERAL PRINCIPLES OF MANAGEMENT

(1) Division of work
(2) Authority and responsibility
(3) Discipline
(4) Unity of command
(5) Unity of direction
(6) Subordination of individual interest to general interest
(7) Remuneration of personnel
(8) Centralization
(9) Scalar chain
(10) Order
(11) Equity
(12) Stability of tenure of personnel
(13) Initiative
(14) Esprit de corps

30. CHANGE

Bringing about change is perhaps attempted more often, and yet less well understood, than anything else the supervisor does. How do people generally react to change? (People tend to resist change that is imposed upon them by other individuals or circumstances.

Change is characteristic of every situation. It is a part of every real endeavor where the efforts of people are concerned.

A. Why do people resist change?
   People may resist change because of:
   (1) Fear of the unknown
   (2) Implied criticism
   (3) Unpleasant experiences in the past
   (4) Fear of loss of status
   (5) Threat to the ego
   (6) Fear of loss of economic stability

B. How can we best overcome the resistance to change?
   In initiating change, take these steps:
   (1) Get ready to sell
   (2) Identify sources of help
   (3) Anticipate objections
   (4) Sell benefits
   (5) Listen in depth
   (6) Follow up

B. BRIEF TOPICAL SUMMARIES

I. WHO/WHAT IS THE SUPERVISOR?
   1. The supervisor is often called the "highest level employee and the lowest level manager."
   2. A supervisor is a member of both management and the work group. He acts as a bridge between the two.
   3. Most problems in supervision are in the area of human relations, or people problems.
   4. Employees expect: Respect, opportunity to learn and to advance, and a sense of belonging, and so forth.
   5. Supervisors are responsible for directing people and organizing work. Planning is of paramount importance.
   6. A position description is a set of duties and responsibilities inherent to a given position.
   7. It is important to keep the position description up-to-date and to provide each employee with his own copy.

II. THE SOCIOLOGY OF WORK
   1. People are alike in many ways; however, each individual is unique.
   2. The supervisor is challenged in getting to know employee differences. Acquiring skills in evaluating individuals is an asset.
   3. Maintaining meaningful working relationships in the organization is of great importance.
   4. The supervisor has an obligation to help individuals to develop to their fullest potential.
   5. Job rotation on a planned basis helps to build versatility and to maintain interest and enthusiasm in work groups.
   6. Cross training (job rotation) provides backup skills.
   7. The supervisor can help reduce tension by maintaining a sense of humor, providing guidance to employees, and by making reasonable and timely decisions. Employees respond favorably to working under reasonably predictable circumstances.
   8. Change is characteristic of all managerial behavior. The supervisor must adjust to changes in procedures, new methods, technological changes, and to a number of new and sometimes challenging situations.
   9. To overcome the natural tendency for people to resist change, the supervisor should become more skillful in initiating change.

III. PRINCIPLES AND PRACTICES OF SUPERVISION
1. Employees should be required to answer to only one superior.
2. A supervisor can effectively direct only a limited number of employees, depending upon the complexity, variety, and proximity of the jobs involved.
3. The organizational chart presents the organization in graphic form. It reflects lines of authority and responsibility as well as interrelationships of units within the organization.
4. Distribution of work can be improved through an analysis using the "Work Distribution Chart."
5. The "Work Distribution Chart" reflects the division of work within a unit in understandable form.
6. When related tasks are given to an employee, he has a better chance of increasing his skills through training.
7. The individual who is given the responsibility for tasks must also be given the appropriate authority to insure adequate results.
8. The supervisor should delegate repetitive, routine work. Preparation of recurring reports, maintaining leave and attendance records are some examples.
9. Good discipline is essential to good task performance. Discipline is reflected in the actions of employees on the job in the absence of supervision.
10. Disciplinary action may have to be taken when the positive aspects of discipline have failed. Reprimand, warning, and suspension are examples of disciplinary action.
11. If a situation calls for a reprimand, be sure it is deserved and remember it is to be done in private.

IV. DYNAMIC LEADERSHIP
1. A style is a personal method or manner of exerting influence.
2. Authoritarian leaders often see themselves as the source of power and authority.
3. The democratic leader often perceives the group as the source of authority and power.
4. Supervisors tend to do better when using the pattern of leadership that is most natural for them.
5. Social scientists suggest that the effective supervisor use the leadership style that best fits the problem or circumstances involved.
6. All four styles -- telling, selling, consulting, joining -- have their place. Using one does not preclude using the other at another time.
7. The theory X point of view assumes that the average person dislikes work, will avoid it whenever possible, and must be coerced to achieve organizational objectives.
8. The theory Y point of view assumes that the average person considers work to be as natural as play, and, when the individual is committed, he requires little supervision or direction to accomplish desired objectives.
9. The leader's basic assumptions concerning human behavior and human nature affect his actions, decisions, and other managerial practices.
10. Dissatisfaction among employees is often present, but difficult to isolate. The supervisor should seek to weaken dissatisfaction by keeping promises, being sincere and considerate, keeping employees informed, and so forth.
11. Constructive suggestions should be encouraged during the natural progress of the work.

V. PROCESSES FOR SOLVING PROBLEMS
1. People find their daily tasks more meaningful and satisfying when they can improve them.
2. The causes of problems, or the key factors, are often hidden in the background. Ability to solve problems often involves the ability to isolate them from their backgrounds. There is some substance to the cliché that some persons "can't see the forest for the trees."
3. New procedures are often developed from old ones. Problems should be broken down into manageable parts. New ideas can be adapted from old ones.

4. People think differently in problem-solving situations. Using a logical, patterned approach is often useful. One approach found to be useful includes these steps:
    (a) Define the problem   (d) Weigh and decide
    (b) Establish objectives   (e) Take action
    (c) Get the facts   (f) Evaluate action

VI. TRAINING FOR RESULTS

1. Participants respond best when they feel training is important to them.
2. The supervisor has responsibility for the training and development of those who report to him.
3. When training is delegated to others, great care must be exercised to insure the trainer has knowledge, aptitude, and interest for his work as a trainer.
4. Training (learning) of some type goes on continually. The most successful supervisor makes certain the learning contributes in a productive manner to operational goals.
5. New employees are particularly susceptible to training. Older employees facing new job situations require specific training, as well as having need for development and growth opportunities.
6. Training needs require continuous monitoring.
7. The training officer of an agency is a professional with a responsibility to assist supervisors in solving training problems.
8. Many of the self-development steps important to the supervisor's own growth are equally important to the development of peers and subordinates. Knowledge of these is important when the supervisor consults with others on development and growth opportunities.

VII. HEALTH, SAFETY, AND ACCIDENT PREVENTION

1. Management-minded supervisors take appropriate measures to assist employees in maintaining health and in assuring safe practices in the work environment.
2. Effective safety training and practices help to avoid injury and accidents.
3. Safety should be a management goal. All infractions of safety which are observed should be corrected without exception.
4. Employees' safety attitude, training and instruction, provision of safe tools and equipment, supervision, and leadership are considered highly important factors which contribute to safety and which can be influenced directly by supervisors.
5. When accidents do occur they should be investigated promptly for very important reasons, including the fact that information which is gained can be used to prevent accidents in the future.

VIII. EQUAL EMPLOYMENT OPPORTUNITY

1. The supervisor should endeavor to treat all employees fairly, without regard to religion, race, sex, or national origin.
2. Groups tend to reflect the attitude of the leader. Prejudice can be detected even in very subtle form. Supervisors must strive to create a feeling of mutual respect and confidence in every employee.
3. Complete utilization of all human resources is a national goal. Equitable consideration should be accorded women in the work force, minority-group members, the physically and mentally handicapped, and the older employee. The important question is: "Who can do the job?"
4. Training opportunities, recognition for performance, overtime assignments, promotional opportunities, and all other personnel actions are to be handled on an equitable basis.

IX. IMPROVING COMMUNICATIONS

1. Communications is achieving understanding between the sender and the receiver of a message. It also means sharing information -- the creation of understanding.
2. Communication is basic to all human activity. Words are means of conveying meanings; however, real meanings are in people.
3. There are very practical differences in the effectiveness of one-way, impersonal, and two-way communications. Words spoken face-to-face are better understood. Telephone conversations are effective, but lack the rapport of person-to-person exchanges. The whole person communicates.
4. Cooperation and communication in an organization go hand in hand. When there is a mutual respect between people, spelling out rules and procedures for communicating is unnecessary.
5. There are several barriers to effective communications. These include failure to listen with respect and understanding, lack of skill in feedback, and misinterpreting the meanings of words used by the speaker. It is also common practice to listen to what we want to hear, and tune out things we do not want to hear.
6. Communication is management's chief problem. The supervisor should accept the challenge to communicate more effectively and to improve interagency and intra-agency communications.
7. The supervisor may often plan for and conduct meetings. The planning phase is critical and may determine the success or the failure of a meeting.
8. Speaking before groups usually requires extra effort. Stage fright may never disappear completely, but it can be controlled.

X. SELF-DEVELOPMENT

1. Every employee is responsible for his own self-development.
2. Toastmaster and toastmistress clubs offer opportunities to improve skills in oral communications.
3. Planning for one's own self-development is of vital importance. Supervisors know their own strengths and limitations better than anyone else.
4. Many opportunities are open to aid the supervisor in his developmental efforts, including job assignments; training opportunities, both governmental and non-governmental -- to include universities and professional conferences and seminars.
5. Programmed instruction offers a means of studying at one's own rate.
6. Where difficulties may arise from a supervisor's being away from his work for training, he may participate in televised home study or correspondence courses to meet his self-develop- ment needs.

XI. TEACHING AND TRAINING

A. The Teaching Process

Teaching is encouraging and guiding the learning activities of students toward established goals. In most cases this process consists in five steps: preparation, presentation, summarization, evaluation, and application.

1. Preparation

    Preparation is twofold in nature; that of the supervisor and the employee.

    Preparation by the supervisor is absolutely essential to success. He must know what, when, where, how, and whom he will teach. Some of the factors that should be considered are:

    (1) The objectives
    (2) The materials needed
    (3) The methods to be used
    (4) Employee participation
    (5) Employee interest
    (6) Training aids
    (7) Evaluation
    (8) Summarization

Employee preparation consists in preparing the employee to receive the material. Probably the most important single factor in the preparation of the employee is arousing and maintaining his interest. He must know the objectives of the training, why he is there, how the material can be used, and its importance to him.

2. Presentation

In presentation, have a carefully designed plan and follow it.
The plan should be accurate and complete, yet flexible enough to meet situations as they arise. The method of presentation will be determined by the particular situation and objectives.

3. Summary

A summary should be made at the end of every training unit and program. In addition, there may be internal summaries depending on the nature of the material being taught. The important thing is that the trainee must always be able to understand how each part of the new material relates to the whole.

4. Application

The supervisor must arrange work so the employee will be given a chance to apply new knowledge or skills while the material is still clear in his mind and interest is high. The trainee does not really know whether he has learned the material until he has been given a chance to apply it. If the material is not applied, it loses most of its value.

5. Evaluation

The purpose of all training is to promote learning. To determine whether the training has been a success or failure, the supervisor must evaluate this learning.
In the broadest sense evaluation includes all the devices, methods, skills, and techniques used by the supervisor to keep him self and the employees informed as to their progress toward the objectives they are pursuing. The extent to which the employee has mastered the knowledge, skills, and abilities, or changed his attitudes, as determined by the program objectives, is the extent to which instruction has succeeded or failed.
Evaluation should not be confined to the end of the lesson, day, or program but should be used continuously. We shall note later the way this relates to the rest of the teaching process.

B. Teaching Methods

A teaching method is a pattern of identifiable student and instructor activity used in presenting training material.
All supervisors are faced with the problem of deciding which method should be used at a given time.
As with all methods, there are certain advantages and disadvantages to each method.

1. Lecture

The lecture is direct oral presentation of material by the supervisor. The present trend is to place less emphasis on the trainer's activity and more on that of the trainee.

2. Discussion

Teaching by discussion or conference involves using questions and other techniques to arouse interest and focus attention upon certain areas, and by doing so creating a learning situation. This can be one of the most valuable methods because it gives the employees 'an opportunity to express their ideas and pool their knowledge.

3. Demonstration

The demonstration is used to teach how something works or how to do something. It can be used to show a principle or what the results of a series of actions will be. A well-staged demonstration is particularly effective because it shows proper methods of performance in a realistic manner.

4. Performance

Performance is one of the most fundamental of all learning techniques or teaching methods. The trainee may be able to tell how a specific operation should be performed but he cannot be sure he knows how to perform the operation until he has done so.

5. Which Method to Use

Moreover, there are other methods and techniques of teaching. It is difficult to use any method without other methods entering into it. In any learning situation a combination of methods is usually more effective than anyone method alone.

Finally, evaluation must be integrated into the other aspects of the teaching-learning process.

It must be used in the motivation of the trainees; it must be used to assist in developing understanding during the training; and it must be related to employee application of the results of training.

This is distinctly the role of the supervisor.